LUCKY GEORGE

LUCKY

The Unforgettable Adventures of a Free-lance Photographer

GEORGE

For Wholesale/Distributor
orders, please contact:

Baker & Taylor
www.btol.com
Phone: 800.775.1800

or

Ingram Content Group, Inc.
www.ingramcontent.com
Phone: 615.793.5000

For individual orders, go to:
www.amazon.com/dp/1482764962

or

www.createspace.com/4125773

or visit

www.luckygeorgethebook.com

George Kufrin's photography
is represented by:
Berlanga Fine Art ~ Photographs
230 W. Superior Street, First Floor
Chicago, Illinois 60654
Phone: 773.255.4031
http://paulberlanga.com

© 2012 George Kufrin | American Studio Press
ISBN: 10: 148-2764962
ISBN: 13: 978-1482764963

For my father, Paul Kelečić Kufrin, an artist and a survivor.

And for my son, Ben Marco Kufrin, who has his grandfather's spirit and his talent.

ACKNOWLEDGMENTS

I want to thank the following people who were and are important in my life:

My long-time friend, Mike Shea, who taught me how to use a Speed Graphic camera;

Leonard Lambs Serdiuk, the editor and publisher of the *West Side News,* who took a chance and gave me my first free-lance job as a news photographer;

Vern Whaley and Don Alford, who launched me into the national news business;

Billy Goat Sianis, who let me and my Speed Graphic hang out in his tavern at 1855 W. Madison Street, with all the big-time news people, and never once asked for my ID;

Carl Snyder, who involved me (and him) in the wonderful world of wild animals and movie stars;

Master Sergeant Nicolas Nicaten, who kept me out of the stockade during Korea;

Bobby Kotalik, who gave me a roof over my head when I really needed it;

Sam Lyons and Mohan Lewis who introduced me to the world of high finance, millionaires and the experience of traveling "first class" around the country;

Don Alford, again, who hounded me until I called Prudential, which turned out to be one of the best calls of my life;

Edna Snyder and Carla Snyder Belniak for their long, loyal and rollicking friendship;

Author and historian, Lila Weinberg, who enthusiastically urged me to write this book years ago but did not live to see it;

Using only the manuscript and stacks of photographs, designer Bob Feie created this book, a process he had to convince me would happen, and I'll be ever grateful that he did;

Fredi Mohr Leaf, the artist who changed my life forever and for the better when she introduced me to Joan, who married me;

And finally, Joan, without whom there would be no book. She made me learn how to use a computer to write it. Then researched and checked my facts, corrected the spelling and edited the book into what you're reading.

I love you all and appreciate everything you've done for me.

George Kufrin
November 29, 2012

Contents

Preface

I was born on Christmas Day, 1926. Not in a manger but in Saint Anthony's Hospital in Chicago. My mother cried for two days because she had her heart set on a girl she could name Gloria, after her favorite movie star Gloria Swanson.

Many years later I photographed Ms. Swanson in Chicago. She was between trains and on her way to New York to promote her latest movie, *Sunset Boulevard*. When I found out I was to photograph her, I debated with myself whether to tell her that story.

Then I met her. I was introduced as "the new photographer." She was dressed to the hilt and looked every bit the movie star. She thanked me for being there, wished me well in my career, and hoped we would meet again. Real class.

I said nothing about my birth.

So why am I so lucky? I believe more exciting events happened during my lifetime than in any period in history, and I was lucky to witness them or to be in the middle of them. Though I missed the Roaring '20s, from the Great Depression on I never had a dull moment. Maybe not always good moments, but never dull.

As a little kid I was interested in photography and I could take pictures better than most. So in high school I got serious and decided to be a professional. In those

George Kufrin, 1944 (Photo by Mike Shea)

good old days, all it took to go pro was to print up business cards with a picture of a camera and my phone number on it. No licenses, tax forms, or permits.

My neighborhood paper, the *West Side News,* gave me my start. I was 16. They paid me two dollars a picture, I furnished the film and flash bulbs, and I was on my way. I never dreamed it would lead to meeting and photographing hundreds of movie and TV stars, sports greats, writers, politicians, bank presidents and CEOs, and two U.S. presidents, John F. Kennedy and Jimmy Carter.

During the past few years I've found that whenever I go to a party or a dinner, the talk usually gets around to the "good old days." Someone will say they liked Burt Lancaster in *"The Killers"* or in *"Atlantic City."* And I'll say, "When I photographed Burt at the Oriental Theatre, he was doing his acrobatic act on stage. His partner would hold a long pole, two stories high, and Burt would climb to the top and do his routine up there. From my standpoint, it really looked dangerous, but Burt told me he loved doing it."

Or I'll mention when I was 17 my Speed Graphic camera assured me entrance to both the Republican and Democratic national conventions of 1944 at the Chicago Stadium. Afterward, I would hang out at the (original) Billy Goat Inn across the street where I drank beer with big-time news people. Life was beautiful.

Or I'll tell them about the time I drove Danny Thomas to a farm outside Chicago to photograph him with a cow (publicizing milk for a local dairy). On the way back, my new car got a flat tire. At the time, Danny was appearing at Chicago's famous Chez Paree. One of his funniest stories: A man has a flat tire and walks a mile to borrow a jack. At each step he gets madder, imagining how much the gas station will charge him. So mad that when he gets there, he yells, "Keep your #%& jack, you crook!"

Luckily, I had a jack, and Danny Thomas wasn't like his imaginary character. Not only did he help me change the tire, he bought me dinner and the show at the Chez. If you never saw Danny Thomas's nightclub act, you missed the best.

After a few stories like that, people always want more. And the evening usually ends with someone saying, "You should write a book!"

So I did. And this is it.

Danny Thomas, 1949

George Kufrin's parents, Paul and Mae (Mary) Kufrin, circa 1918

CHAPTER ONE

I Was Born

My father, Paul Kufrin, was a very successful sculptor in the '20s. And though he was born and educated in Croatia,[1] he knew more American history than most Americans. He constantly quoted from memory the words of George Washington, Thomas Jefferson and, especially, Thomas Paine. In 1906, at the age of 19, he emigrated to the United States, the country he had loved and admired his entire life.

In those days, sculptors were in great demand. He traveled all over the United States creating statues and ornamental work for the splendid new theaters and commercial buildings going up everywhere. Some of those buildings are still standing.

When he married my mother, Mary Vejvoda, in 1919, my father settled in Chicago and opened his own studio. He named it the American Studio to honor his adopted country.

It was a huge place on Ogden Avenue near Cook County Hospital, with high ceilings and skylights. Plaster and molds were everywhere, and there was plenty of clay to play with. Going there was my idea of major fun.

Life was good. The American Studio, with several employees, thrived. My father bought a Willys Knight sedan that we would take on picnics to the Forest Preserves around Chicago. He really loved that car. There was even a triumphant trip back to Europe for my parents, first-class, on the Aquitania.

[1] Royal Academy of Fine Arts of Zagreb, Croatia

(left to right) The American Studio, circa 1922; Paul Kufrin with his bust of Anton Cermak, circa 1931

But in a few years it was all gone. First, the stock market crash of 1929 hit my father hard. The final blow was the bank holiday of 1933. My father had deposited a large check in his bank for a job he had just completed, ironically, for another bank, the day before President Roosevelt closed all the banks. Overnight, he was literally wiped out. This, coupled with a national cessation of new building construction, put him out of business.

I was old enough to realize there was trouble but too young to remember much of the good days so it didn't hit me as hard as it did my parents. I'm surprised they survived as well as they did. We moved a couple of times, each time to a smaller flat. The last one we settled in for the rest of the Depression was a very small, dark, two-bedroom flat, heated by a large coal-burning stove situated in the middle of the kitchen, the largest room.

We went on relief. They didn't call it welfare then, and if you were on it you were ashamed to let anyone else know. They didn't send relief checks. They sent a truck with canned goods and bags of beans and rice and flour.

A case worker made surprise visits to make sure we were still poor. I would have to hide the dog. Relief families weren't allowed dogs—or telephones or cars.

Eventually, my father got a job with the W.P.A. (Works Progress Administration), a government-funded arts program created by FDR to help artists and art programs during the Depression. Artists applied to a panel of their peers, had to show evidence of their training, experience and ability, and, if accepted for an assignment, would be paid $23 to $35 a week to complete it. My father hated the process but was happy to be working.

My mother landed a job in a clothing store on Maxwell Street, an exciting place in the '30s. On weekends, it bustled with mostly Jewish immigrants who lined their pushcarts and stands next to each other and sold everything you could think of, all of it wholesale. There were also permanent stores that sold clothing and hardware. One of the most important employees in my mother's store was the "puller." His job was to give a sales spiel to passersby as he physically pulled them into the store. I'd like to see someone try that today.

I once asked my mother why those Gypsy ladies on Maxwell Street were sitting in the store windows. She said, "Selling costumes." Everything was for sale.

Things eventually got a little better economically for our family. We got a phone and I didn't have to hide the dog. But the best part was that we always stayed in the same neighborhood. And what a great neighborhood it was. Made up of about 90 percent Bohemian immigrants who settled in the same area of Chicago, we were the famous 22nd ward on the city's far West side. My mother was one of these immigrants. She came to America with her family from Bohemia, now the Czech Republic, in 1906.

I was able to stay in the same grammar school—Robert Burns—and the same high school—David Glasgow Farragut—with the same friends, all the way up to World War II. I still keep in touch with some of them.

What made the neighborhood great was its economic diversity. I lived a block from Mayor Anton Cermak. Down the street lived the local bank president and across the street a judge. In between were factory workers, policemen, firemen, artists, musicians, school teachers and politicians. I'd never again see a neighborhood where people of every economic status lived together and got along.

There were some people in my neighborhood the Depression didn't affect, but not many. The good jobs went to policemen and firemen. You had to have a politician sponsor you to get one of those. People who were unemployed were always looking for odd jobs to make some money.

Like the lady pastry chef who worked in Vienna before coming to this country. My father, trying to hold on to his beloved Willys Knight, put it up on blocks in her garage. She charged him 25 cents a month for storage.

She was always making the most wonderful strudel in the world. I don't know where she sold it, but I know she didn't eat it all. Whenever I came with the 25 cents storage rent, she'd give me a piece of the strudel. My father finally had to sell his car and that was the end of the strudel. I shudder when I think how little he sold the car for.

When I walked to grammar school, I passed the Kraml Dairy, which was in the middle of a residential block. This small dairy had a store in front and a stable in the rear where they kept their horses and wagons for delivering milk. On my way, I usually went in back to pet the horses.

There was also a very nice butcher shop on the corner of our block. It was small but well equipped with large coolers, chopping blocks, saws and many knives. Whenever I was sent to the butcher to buy meat, I would take my dog Queenie with me. I never bought much, but each time the butcher would give my dog a piece of meat or a bone, usually with more meat on it than what I was buying. Such a nice man but he always looked sad.

One day when I went to the butcher's shop it was locked with a "Closed" sign on the door. My mother said he went out of business. It was the height of the Depression so that wasn't so unusual. I found out later the butcher had hanged himself.

Not long after that happened I came home from school and couldn't find Queenie. My mother said, "That dog has chewed her last shoe and her last piece of furniture!" She had told my brother to take Queenie to the dog pound.

I was in shock. The pound was about a mile from our flat. I raced down there and cried my eyes out. They gave Queenie back to me and didn't even make me buy a license for her, which of course we couldn't afford anyway. When we got home, I promised my mother that Queenie wouldn't chew any more furniture. And Queenie stayed.

There were a lot of cheap things you could do during the Depression. My mother always worked on Sundays but my father didn't. He'd often take me to Navy Pier on the streetcar. Kids' fare, three cents. Adults,' seven cents.

Today, Navy Pier is a huge entertainment center with theaters, rides, restaurants, and cruise ships sailing from it. Then, it was a giant warehouse with some exhibition halls. At the end of the pier was a great domed building that stills stands. But it was open air then. Concerts were played there, and dances took place on the weekends. There were also speedboat rides, a penny arcade, and hot dog stands. I was seven years old and I thought Navy Pier was the greatest place in the world.

Whenever he could, my father would exhibit his work, and we'd visit the galleries downtown where his sculpture was shown. One of the biggest shows was at Navy Pier, where his sculpture of *"The American Indian"* was the hit of the show.

However by far, the most important event in the '30s was the Chicago World's Fair—A Century of Progress—in 1933. My father's bust of *"Clarence Darrow"* was awarded the Gold Medal for sculpture at the Fair's Illinois Pavilion. His *"American Indian"* was also exhibited there. Because he had an exhibitor's pass, we went to the Fair early and often. I'll never forget it.

I watched the Ford Motor Company's exhibit of a small assembly line build a car before your eyes. Ford also displayed a "talking convertible" covered with sequins that told the crowds about the Ford Motor Company.

Chrysler gave free rides in its new car that had an all-steel roof. A can company made and gave away cans that were actually little banks. A movie company demonstrated how movies were made. There were other shows, but they were not for kids. I did see Sally Rand, but she was outside the theatre and demurely clothed.

Hawkers were everywhere. I bought my first camera from one of them. It cost 25 cents and when I got it home it didn't work. A bit later I got another, better camera. Free. It was a Bob Hope camera that you got for buying Pepsodent toothpaste.

"The American Indian" *by Paul Kufrin, 1932 (Photo by Chicago Architectural Photographing Co.)*

A major Fair attraction was the Skyride. There were two very tall towers named Amos and Andy after the two popular radio characters. Cable cars ran between them. The cars were named The Kingfish, Madam Queen, and other characters from that radio show.

All seven-year-olds should have a World's Fair in their childhood.

What they shouldn't have is a ruptured appendix. One afternoon, while my brother and I were taking turns jumping off the living room couch, I felt the most terrific pain in my side that wouldn't stop. Our family doctor, Dr. Frank Jirka, rushed to the house, did a brief exam and told my folks to get me to Cook County Hospital. *Fast*. In spite of the awful pain, I was excited to go because it would be my first taxi ride.

In the hospital ward after the operation, I heard nurses whispering about my chances. They weren't good. I was full of infection and these were the days before penicillin.

For two weeks I lay under a heat tent over my stomach designed to draw all the poisons out of my system. It worked. I finally recovered and went home, the first —but not last—lucky break I would have in my life.

Another huge event of 1933 was the shooting of Chicago Mayor Anton Cermak while he was in Miami with President Franklin Roosevelt. They were sitting in an open car when the assassin ran up and tried to shoot Roosevelt. He missed and shot the mayor instead. Cermak died a few days later. It was widely reported that Cermak's last words were, "I'm glad it was me instead of you." But more than one person, including me, still believes that the assassin in Miami hit his main target.

Cermak was laid out in his home on Millard Avenue, around the corner from where I lived. Thousands of people filed past his casket, including me. I think more neighbors were interested in seeing the inside of the mayor's house than in actually seeing him. After a long wait, I got to the casket but I was too short to see in. Someone lifted me up. The coffin had a glass top but I had a good look. The mayor was really dead.

After Cermak's death, the Irish pretty much took over the Chicago political machine that Cermak started. The next mayor was Edward J. Kelly, the first of five mayors from Bridgeport. During his tenure, Soldier Field was built.

Later, Otto Kerner, a federal judge and a good Bohemian, married Cermak's daughter Eleanor and moved into Cermak's big house. At that time, I was delivering their newspapers. I remember Kerner coming to the door in his bathrobe when I came to collect for the papers.

After Cermak, Kerner was the pride of the Bohemians. He would later become governor of Illinois. He was well-liked but was convicted of bribery and other counts connected to Arlington and Washington Park Race Tracks receiving choice racing dates while he was governor. He went to prison for three years, sent there by prosecutor James R. Thompson, a future Illinois governor.

During those days, everyone was trying to make a buck and I was no different. People laugh at me today when I tell them that I sold doughnuts and made change when I was five. It's true. But don't feel sorry for me. I thought it was fun. After working my way up from doughnuts, I sold magazines door-to-door ("Lady, would you please buy a *Ladies' Home Companion?*"), shined shoes in taverns, and had a newspaper route.

One Christmas when I was 10 or 11, I got a Christmas present I really wanted: a Home Foundry Kit. It consisted of two steel molds with wooden handles held together with a clamp. Also included were a ladle on a stand and some lead pellets. The instructions were to clamp the molds together, put the ladle with pellets in it over a burner on the kitchen range until the pellets melted. Then pour the molten lead into the mold. When the lead hardened, you would remove the clamp and you'd have three lead soldiers.

I was in heaven making lead soldiers, standing on a chair at my mother's kitchen range. The only bad part was that they only gave you enough lead for about a dozen soldiers. More lead cost extra.

But luckily a schoolmate's father who lived across the street was replacing the water pipes in his house. The old lead pipes were lying around their back yard. He said, "Help yourself." I soon had a lead soldier factory. My lead soldiers are gone now but every once in a while one will turn up among some old keepsakes.

I haven't seen the Home Foundry Kit in toy stores lately. I wonder why.

When I was in eighth grade, a man from the Chicago Musical Instrument Company came to our front door selling musical instruments and lessons. Was there a special instrument I was interested in? Of course, I told him. The trumpet.

It was the era of the big bands. Whenever I could, I'd go downtown to hear one. They performed on stage at either the Chicago or Oriental Theatre or at live radio broadcasts. I thought trumpet players were the best and Harry James was my idol. He had played with the Benny Goodman orchestra and then gone on to form his own band.

James had a radio show sponsored by Chesterfield cigarettes. At one of his broadcasts from the Civic Opera House, all of us kids received a free pack of cigarettes afterward. Different times.

I heard Les Brown and his great band do a broadcast, sponsored by Fitch Shampoo, from the NBC studios atop the Merchandise Mart. I especially liked his new girl singer, Doris Day. But Les didn't give us free shampoo afterward.

Anyway, although it was a hardship, my parents signed me up to buy a trumpet on the installment plan and take the lessons that went with it. That was a great day, because when I went to high school a year later I auditioned for—and got into—the concert band. The band became the highlight of high school for me.

Our bandmaster, Marcel Ackerman, was a stocky guy about eight years older than we were. He wore his black hair slicked straight back, like George Raft, and he went by the name of Boss. A typical note on the blackboard would read: "Brass section practice today 3:00-5:00. (signed) The Boss."

We all loved him, even when he'd hit you on the head with his baton for playing a passage wrong. Music was his life. Though he knew how to have fun, music to him was dead serious. He'd holler when we didn't get it right, but when we did his smile made it all worthwhile.

One day at rehearsal, Rudy Stauber, the first trumpet and a very large guy, played a difficult solo brilliantly. After he finished, Ackerman looked at us all and sighed. "And I wanted him to play the tuba." Rudy and several of the kids in the band later became professional musicians and music teachers.

George Kufrin at post-Band Concert festivities, 1943 (Photo by Mike Shea)

We played all the great classical composers from Beethoven to Mahler to, of course, Bohemian Antonin Dvorak. Also the rousing marches of John Phillips Sousa and modern works by George Gershwin and Aaron Copeland. When we did the *"1812 Overture"* we didn't have a cannon, so a man backstage shot off a blank pistol. It worked.

Every year the City of Chicago held a competition for high school bands. Even though we were a small school, we always entered the highest category: 90 pieces or larger. And that's when we really worked. Ackerman would rehearse the band, section by section, instrument by instrument, and he would get you out of class if you needed more rehearsal. We were the pride of Farragut High School. We won every competition we entered and had the highest rating in the city.

I'll always be grateful to The Boss for teaching me to appreciate good music. It was a very sad day when he was drafted into the army. And the graduating seniors in the band were not far behind him.

For me, high school was a busy time. Besides the band, I always had a job. Either I was setting pins in a bowling alley, delivering flowers, filling orders at Montgomery Ward's mail-order house or doing photo finishing for a company that serviced drugstores. One summer I got a job at the Union Stock Yards for Armour & Co. I worked in a building where the pigs walked in one end and came out in cans at the other.

I made enough money that summer to buy a Speed Graphic camera. Now I was a real photographer. How could a camera be the major influence in my life? I'll tell you. A Speed Graphic is the big bulky camera with bellows that you see in all the old movies when the photographers rush into the courtroom and start firing flash bulbs.

If you had a Speed Graphic no one asked you for credentials. When they saw that camera, they held the door open for you. If I went to a fire or a car wreck or any disaster that was roped off, I would crawl under the rope and ask the nearest cop, "What's going on here?" or "Who's in charge?" No one asked who I was. They saw the camera and figured I belonged.

I bought the camera in 1943. Although still in high school, I was working for the neighborhood newspaper. I got two dollars a picture and I furnished the film and flashbulbs and made the prints. In between shooting news I shot weddings every weekend. I loved shooting weddings. I met a lot of bridesmaids. I was happy. I was making money. And I thought I was a real operator.

What I didn't know was that Speed Graphic camera was going to change my life.

One October night, I was parked with a girlfriend behind a neighborhood coal yard listening to the radio. All of a sudden there was this huge fire and the place burned down rapidly. Because I always had my Speed Graphic with me, I got some great pictures. By the time the photographers from the downtown papers got there all they could shoot was a smoldering mess. I had all the flames.

This was too good for the *West Side News*.

I took my girlfriend home and raced downtown to the *Chicago Herald American* to see if I could sell them a picture. They had sent a man to the fire but he got there too late. When I told them I had the flames, they developed the film. They picked the best one, ran it full page, and sent it upstairs to International News Photos (INP) to put on the syndicate wire. It was Friday, the 13th of October, 1944. I was in heaven.

The next morning I went back to the paper to see about getting paid. That's when I met Vern Whaley, the picture editor and a Chicago newspaper legend. He congratulated me on the picture. I was impressed when he called me "pal." I didn't realize he called everyone "pal." He looked a lot like Ernie Kovak, with the big black mustache. He promised the check would be in the mail.

I called him a couple of weeks later to see what had happened to the check. He told me to come down and he would have it for me. I went and he had the check. Sixteen dollars. I wasn't too disappointed because in 1944 you could buy a pound of coffee for 30 cents or a loaf of bread for ten cents. I was just happy to be in the big time. When Vern asked me what I was doing, I told him I was a free-lancer, but I'd be going into the Merchant Marines in January, after I graduated from high school.

Vern told me to look him up after the war because he had a little picture business across the street in the Civic Opera Building and that sometimes when it got busy he used free-lancers. I said I would, never dreaming that this was the start of a friendship that lasted almost 50 years.

In the meantime, if there was a big football game on Saturday, I'd shoot it for the school or the *West Side News*. This called for a visit to Isadore Dobkin's photo supply house on Kedzie Avenue, which he owned with his daughter, Goldie. Isadore had sold me my Speed Graphic and I continued to buy all my film and other supplies from him.

Isadore supplied a lot of photographers, especially those we called kidnappers. These guys went door-to-door taking pictures of babies and small kids, a big business then. If you had a pony to set the kid on you did even better. It was fun hang-

Coal Burns—but in Wrong Place

Chicago Herald American, *Friday, October 13, 1944* *(Herald-American International photo)*

ing around the store and listening to kidnappers' stories. But it was a hard way to make a living and none of them could do it for very long.

Anyway, on many Friday afternoons, I went to Isadore's to tell him I was thinking of buying the 4x5 Graflex camera he had on the shelf. I'd like to try it out over the weekend. He was a great guy. And he usually loaned me the camera.

At the time, the Graflex was the best camera for shooting sports even though it looked kind of odd. It had a big hood on top that you looked down into. With one hand you focused on the action, with the other hand you tripped the shutter. It made a lot of noise when the mirror inside flipped up and the shutter went off. After each picture you had to turn the film holder around and wind up the shutter for the next shot.

It was a great camera. But I always returned it on Monday. Isadore knew I wasn't about to buy it.

He once showed me a new camera that was coming out. He told me it was called a Polaroid. I said, "It'll never catch on." That's how smart I was.

I met Mike Shea during high school at the Camera Club. He was working after school at a camera store owned by a former *Chicago Tribune* photographer, Ed Shiska. Mike already had a Speed Graphic and more experience than I had. We became good friends and were soon sitting up all night listening to the police radio so we could be the first ones to a crime scene or fire.

Mike quit school to do full-time photography. I stayed in school but we got together almost every night. He was a party animal and I tried to keep up with him. Photography always came first but fun ran a close second.

We knew we would be drafted soon so it wasn't a time to make long-term plans. We did a lot of roller-skating and there were many parties for guys leaving for the army and guys coming home on leave. Mike always knew where the next party was. He was a year older than I and was drafted into the Army first. I left almost a year later for the Merchant Marines. It was only after the war that we both got serious about work.

Mike had a great family. His mother's name was Joe (correct spelling) because her father had wanted a boy and he was going to have a Joe one way or the other.

(l-r) GK, Mike Shea and unidentified friend

Mike's father, Pat Shea, was a real Irish character. Pat worked as a cutter in a clothing factory. He was also a tailor. He would bring home ends of gabardine bolts, sometimes pretty long ends, and make special jackets and slacks for Mike and me. The pockets of the jackets were big enough to hold 4x5 film holders and many flash bulbs. Pat didn't believe in zippers so the slacks had buttons. There were times that proved awkward.

Mike and I sometimes worked together or would cover for each other. Mostly we did our own jobs but we still borrowed equipment from each other and shared our active social life.

Mike was into shooting a lot of show biz people. My favorite story is when he had a job to shoot a comedian in a studio. At the time I had a small studio on Division and Clark Streets that Mike was welcome to use. He asked me to help with the shoot. We went to the Palmer House where the comedian was appearing. He was a rising new star named Jonathan Winters. Mike went in to get him and the three of us drove back to my studio. Winters seemed like a nice guy but he didn't talk much and didn't seem too funny.

Back at the studio, we met with the client, Hugh Hefner, who had just started a new magazine called *Playboy*. Hef's right-hand man, Victor Lownes III, was there too. To me, Victor was an authentic, North Shore sophisticated playboy. He was wealthy, drove an MG, found the Playmates for the magazine, started the Playboy Jazz Festival, and was great at locating new talent. Before he joined the magazine, Victor had been doing P.R. for Arnold Morton, at Morton's key club called the Walton Walk, of which I was a member.

We hung a background and Mike got ready to shoot. The idea was for Winters to go through his act while Mike kept shooting the different expressions on his face. Well, he got started and he was terrific. We were all on the floor laughing. Mike had to stop shooting at times because he was laughing so hard he couldn't focus. What a night. I predicted Winters would go far and that *Playboy* would too.

Mike later went into motion picture photography and became a successful cinematographer for commercials and movies. He moved to Hollywood where he was killed in a helicopter crash filming aerial shots for a music video at age 70.

One morning, my mother looked out the window and yelled that she was going to call the police. Someone had parked an old junk car in front of our house. I had to tell her the car was mine. It was a 1927 Chrysler that I bought for 20 dollars. It didn't run all the time, so eventually I sold it to Mike's father, Pat, for 50 dollars. He lined the roof with fine gabardine and enjoyed the car for several years.

With the 50 dollars I bought a 1935 Ford coupe. A real press car. I put a large, red sign in the window that said "Press Photographer."

I was really hot stuff but I was well aware we were at war. I photographed many soldiers and sailors shipping out and, sadly, too many memorials.

GK and 1935 Ford "Press" car (Photo by Hank Patula)

The war also meant many items were rationed, including gas and photographic materials. Because I worked for the *West Side News,* I had priorities for both.

I made friends with many of the photographers on the big daily papers. One of them, George Kotalik of the *Chicago Times,* became famous for a picture he

*(l-r) Betty Mae Belinski, GK, Audrey Sobel
and his first car, a '27 Chrysler, 1943
(Photo by Mike Shea)*

took on December 7, 1941. He climbed up the outside of the Japanese Consulate building at night and, through the window, took a picture of the Japanese consul, in his underwear, burning records. It was called "Honorable Jap Caught with Pants Down." George won many awards for it.

One day, George said we could make some good money taking pictures of patrons in a nightclub that belonged to a friend of his. The Club Charming. Charming it wasn't. It was a big, rough, strip joint on the North Side. During the war, places like this were very popular. He said we could set up a darkroom in the basement. He had a man to work in the darkroom and we would take the pictures.

I was important to the project because I had the film and the flashbulbs and owned an enlarger. Nick, the darkroom man, would develop the film and make prints from the wet negatives. The people would get their prints in a half hour.

We had a lot of people come down to the darkroom and pay double to destroy the negatives. It seemed not everyone was there with his wife. One night, a man wanted 10 prints of his picture. By the time Nick got to the seventh print, the negative started to melt from the heat of the enlarger. When that happens, the print looks like the picture of Dorian Gray. What do we do now?

I told Nick to make 12 prints and put the good ones on top. It's dark up there. Maybe when he counts them and sees he has two extra, he won't bother to look at them closely. It worked. I was bad. We did this for several nights. We were supposed to give a percentage of the money to the club owner who was an ex-prizefighter. We never seemed to make much money. One night the owner had his bartenders count how many flashbulbs went off. His tally was much higher than ours. We were asked to leave. *Fast.*

George was soon drafted into the Army. After the war, he opened a camera store and did well. He later opened a bar. Eventually he moved to Tucson, Arizona, and opened a nightclub. We remained friends until he died in 1994. I'm still friends with his younger brother, Bob Kotalik, who became a newspaper photographer after the war and who also made quite a name for himself. When the *Chicago Times* and the *Chicago Sun* merged, Bob became chief photographer of the *Chicago Sun-Times.*

Before he retired, Bob told me he was only allowed to hire photographers with a college degree. I thought that was funny because he didn't have one and I don't think any of those early guys did either. Most of them worked as copy boys and hung out at the darkroom until they learned how to operate a Speed Graphic. Then, if they were good and there was an opening, they became photographers. And they were good. It didn't take a genius to operate the camera. But it took a lot of nerve.

I once asked an old veteran the secret of his success. He said, "F.8 and be there!" In other words, you had to be there even when you were not wanted. Some guys specialized in crime stories. I did a few, too. We knew all the cops. (In those days, the press had a very good relationship with the police.) If a suspect tried to cover his face, the cops would uncover him until we got his picture. Some cops were even known to call a photographer directly and tell him about a breaking story. They don't do that anymore.

Bobby Kotalik and I still get together every year in Arizona to talk about the good old days.

Bobby Kotalik, Chicago, Illinois, circa 1946
(Photo by Carmen Reporto)

By 1944, I was also working for another neighborhood newspaper whose territory included the Chicago Stadium. This was when I became very friendly with Billy Goat Sianis, owner of the tavern by the same name. Billy was a great guy, wore a goatee, and really did resemble a goat. As soon as he spoke, you knew he was from Greece.

The match covers for his tavern read, "The Chicago Stadium is across the street from the Billy Goat Inn. 1855 West Madison Street." Billy had it made. Something was always going on at the stadium. Sports, circuses, conventions. All of these events were covered by the press, including me with my Speed Graphic. And where was the nearest place all of us press people could get a drink? In those days, the Billy Goat Inn was just a tavern. No cheeseburgers. Food came years later when Billy moved downtown.

Billy loved publicity. And he treated the press royally. They, in turn, tried to feature him in news stories. If the circus was in town, "Let's get a clown in the tavern!" or "Put Billy in the cage with the lions." One time, they even brought an elephant into the tavern.

I was talking with Billy one night when the head Andy Frain usher from the stadium rushed in with news. Alan Ladd was across the street, shooting a movie. Did Billy want to get a picture with him?

Of course he did. Billy quickly put on a jacket and hat and I grabbed my Speed Graphic. They were shooting a scene in front of the stadium where posters promoted a prizefight that was part of the film. Billy, wearing a loud sports jacket and a straw hat, was introduced to Ladd as a prominent Chicago businessman. I liked Alan Ladd. He was gracious and seemed to enjoy posing for the picture. I was surprised at how short he was, which you couldn't tell from seeing him in the movies.

Billy also had a live goat that lived out in back of the tavern. He'd bring it in for the customers to pet. He liked to go to the tables where there was cash sitting around and feed a dollar bill to the goat. Most people thought it was funny.

I don't know who came up with the idea of taking the goat to the 1945 World Series, but Billy had the best news and P.R. talent in Chicago sitting at his bar and thinking up what we called "stunts."

He bought two tickets to the series. One for him and one for the goat. The Chicago Cubs forbade Billy to bring the goat into Wrigley Field. They said the goat stunk. So Billy put a hex on the Cubs forever more. Of course, all the press was there to record the confrontation. (Last I checked, the Cubs still haven't won a World Series.)

One night I came into the tavern and Billy told me a truck driver had dropped off a sheep. Why? Well, he said, a goat needed a sheep. But it turned out the sheep had died and it was out back by the goat's pen. He asked me, "How are we gonna get rid of it?"

Billy owned a big, shiny Chrysler and I had my beat-up 1935 Ford. Naturally, we put the dead sheep in my trunk, drove out to the boondocks, and dumped it in an empty field by the Sanitary District. My car smelled of dead sheep for months.

At the 1944 Republican convention, Billy put up a sign in front of the tavern that said, NO REPUBLICANS ALLOWED. They came in anyway and demanded drinks, and of course he served them.

I admit that in some areas I'm really dumb. At that convention, I looked forward to photographing Thomas E. Dewey, the famous "New York crime buster, afraid of none." When I saw him, I couldn't believe my eyes. He was like a little doll. I don't think he weighed 90 pounds.

One night at the Republican convention, a woman in a long, dark-blue dress and with her hair in a bun, made a speech, not about G.I. Joe but about G.I. Jim. Everyone was very impressed with her. Many photographers, including me, often don't concentrate on what people are saying because we are busy focusing the camera or thinking about the light or trying not to fall off whatever we're standing on. The next night, I photographed the same woman with a Girl Scout troop. This time she was gorgeous in her tweed suit with a miniskirt and a Hollywood-type hairdo. It was Clare Booth Luce, wife of Henry Luce, founder and publisher of *Time* and *Life* magazines.

One thing about the 1944 Democratic convention I remember clearly. Up until the last day, everyone carried signs that said Roosevelt and Wallace. But when I came in the last day of the convention there wasn't a Roosevelt and Wallace sign anywhere. Now the signs said Roosevelt and Truman. How did they do that? I never could figure politicians.

West Side News *covers*
GK's departure for Merchant Marines, with his parents, 1945
(Photo by George Kotalik)

CHAPTER TWO

The War

On December 25, 1944, I turned 18. I was due to graduate from Farragut High School in January and knew I was about to be drafted. (The draft board allowed a draftee to finish the school semester before drafting him.)

I didn't think I had the personality for the Army so just before my birthday, I joined the Merchant Marines to fulfill my obligation to military service. The fact that the Merchant Marines had the largest number of casualties per capita of any service during the war didn't bother me. I felt invincible. The reason for the high number of casualties was that the Merchant Marines had no special services or support groups. They had some training, and then got on a ship and tried not to sink.

In early January, 1945, I was sent to the U.S. Maritime Service Training Center at Sheepshead Bay in Brooklyn, New York. I had been told that the Merchant Marines were less structured than the Army or Navy but during training we wore uniforms, slept in barracks, and marched.

After the first few weeks of getting used to the new life, I started to really like it. I had never been far from home before, and now I was living in New York on the Atlantic Ocean—within sight of Coney Island.

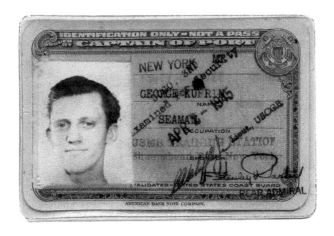

The ship training was hands-on. Our "school" was an exact replica of the deck of a Liberty Ship (with no hull) that had been constructed on the ground. I learned how to work all the rigging, batten down the hatches, tie knots, splice lines, lower lifeboats and everything else that had to do with running the deck. On the mock-up bridge, we learned how to steer the ship.

We didn't have small arms but learned how to fire the five-inch gun, three-inch gun and the four 50-caliber machine guns that a Liberty ship carried on its deck.

We also lowered and sailed lifeboats in Sheepshead Bay. That would have been more fun if it hadn't been January. It's amazing how much you can get into a life-boat—sails, compass, plenty of food and water, and first-aid supplies.

One of the scariest things we did was a swimming drill where we jumped off a 30-foot high platform into a giant indoor swimming pool, came gasping to the surface, splashed water all over our heads as if we were coming up through burning oil and then swam to the lifeboat at the other end of the pool.

After a month of training we were allowed liberty on the weekends. A couple of friends I'd made in maritime school and I set out together to see everything we could of New York City.

I'll never forget coming up out of the BMT subway (fare five cents) into Times Square. It was like landing on the moon. A friendly moon. Everyone was nice to people in uniform.

We decided a good place to start was the Pepsi Cola canteen on 47th Street (in the heart of Times Square) where they gave us free food and all the Pepsi we could drink. Within walking distance was enough activity to last a lifetime. Every weekend after that, I went to Times Square.

Most of the movie theaters in those days had live stage shows between the movies and among the big bands I saw were Benny Goodman, Harry James, Tommy Dorsey, Count Basie, and Les Brown. I also saw entertainers, including Frank Sinatra, at the Paramount. (I couldn't understand why the girls were squealing at this skinny little kid with big ears.)

And no place was more exciting than Radio City Music Hall with the Rockettes, the Corps de Ballet, and the giant revolving stage that went up and down. There was nothing as grand in Chicago. And the best parts? You could sit in the loges and smoke and the drinking age was 18.

I loved New York. There was music everywhere, and I tried to hear it all. The best places to hear it were the row of nightclubs on 52nd St. They were long, narrow spaces with a stand-up bar at the entrance. A person could buy a beer at the bar and nurse it for an hour while listening to great music, a cheap way to hear the best.

One night I was standing at the bar in the Three Deuces, waiting to see Billie Holiday who was appearing there. She was very late. I was on my second beer. When she finally came, she walked in the door and said, "I'm not singing tonight," and walked out. But it wasn't so bad. Also on the bill was Art Tatum.

Easter Sunday, 1945, was quite an event. Fifth Avenue was blocked off in front of St. Patrick's Cathedral. I thought there'd been an accident. When I got closer I found out it was the Easter Parade, an amazing sight. Thousands of people milling around, newsreel cameras on top of station wagons, radio reporters running around with microphones, and, of course, more newspaper reporters and photographers than you'd see at a national convention. Shortly after that event, on May 8, 1945, the war in Europe ended when Germany surrendered.

The length of training at Sheepshead Bay depended on how many ships were being sunk. I was lucky. Since fewer ships were being sunk at the time, I was able

Aboard the Flying Mist, *a C-1 cargo ship bound for Saipan, 1945*

to finish most of my four-month's training. The last thing we did was a week-long training cruise to Baltimore and Chesapeake Bay. When we returned, the orders came down. "Pack your things. You're shipping out tomorrow." I spent five days on a troop train to San Francisco to get a ship to the Pacific war zone.

The sad part of shipping out was that all the friendships you made in training were scattered. Everyone went to different ships. I'd have to make new friends at my next stop. Again I was lucky. My first ship was the *S/S Flying Mist,* a modern cargo ship. I was so happy I wasn't put on a tanker because tankers got blown up quicker. Also, tankers didn't spend as much as time in port. It could take weeks to unload a freighter, but only a couple of hours to unload a tanker. I was assigned to the ship as an AB, an able-bodied seaman.

Again, I was lucky. Though I only had an OS, an ordinary seaman's license, in wartime they make many exceptions. *The Flying Mist* was a beautiful ship, and the crew was something out of an old movie. You want to talk about old salts? Most of them had been sunk at least once, had been in many invasions and spent a lot of time in lifeboats.

They didn't think much of this young punk who was sailing as an AB on his first trip. After a couple of weeks, though, when they realized I knew my job pretty well, we became friends. A merchant ship crew was not like a navy crew back then. We had men of every age, nationality, and race.

The ship was docked in Oakland, California. It took about three weeks to load it, so I got to see a lot of San Francisco. I looked up a family I knew who had moved out there from Chicago. They and their daughter, who was my age, were glad to see me. I would bring them a couple of pounds of butter or other rationed food from the ship, and they showed me the town.

Finally the ship was loaded and ready to sail. It was May 26, 1945. At the last minute our chief steward was replaced because he ordered several cases of vanilla extract. It seems you can get drunk on that, and he had already started.

When a merchant ship is at sea, the ABs and OSs are broken up into three groups of three. Each group stands a four-hour watch with eight hours off every 12 hours. The four hours are broken up into three one-hour, 20-minute segments: one segment at the wheel, one on lookout, and one on standby.

When we got to the Golden Gate Bridge it was my turn at the wheel. As we passed the bridge it was like going over Niagara Falls into a storm to end all storms. The waves were coming over the bridge. I was so seasick I wanted to die. I told the mate I was too sick to steer. He gave me a bucket to vomit in and said, "Shut up and steer."

I was sick for two days. After that, I guess I got my sea stomach because I never got seasick again, even in worse storms crossing the North Atlantic in winter.

After the weather cleared I began to enjoy the beautiful Pacific Ocean. During wartime you are never told where the ship is going. If I was a hotshot spy I could have figured out where we were going because part of our cargo was B-29 engines. And all the B-29s were bombing Japan from their bases in the Mariana Islands. But at the time, I wasn't sharp enough to figure it out, so I didn't know we were going to the Marianas.

The rest of the trip was mostly uneventful except when we would hit a big fish. It made a ping on the sonar, which is the same sound a torpedo makes when it's fired. That would get your attention.

We were not in a convoy, so we zigzagged across the Pacific. That means when you are at the wheel you change course at scattered intervals. The captain sets up a chart of course changes to make. It takes longer to get somewhere, but it's supposed to keep you from being torpedoed.

The Pacific is especially beautiful at night. You can read a book by moonlight. And there is so much phosphorus in the water when the bow cuts through the waves at night it actually looks like it is lit by electricity.

One day at lunch a crew member told me about a time when he was on another ship standing lookout, and he saw a torpedo coming straight at him. He said he was so scared he couldn't open his mouth. I told him I thought that was kind of stupid.

A few nights later, while I was on lookout, I saw what looked like a torpedo coming straight at me with its wake lit up by the phosphorus. I was so scared I couldn't talk. I'm glad I didn't. It was a porpoise. We often had schools of them play around the bow. This one was alone, but the rest of the school soon followed. What a sight.

Our first stop was the island of Eniwetok, a tiny coral atoll in the Marshall Islands. After the battle of the same name in 1944, when American forces captured the 2.5 square mile island from 2,500 Japanese, no trees were left standing and not much of anything else, except a sunken tanker at the mouth of the harbor. We were there only one day and then left for Guam, where we dropped off a couple of navy officer passengers who were to pick up a new ship there. Eniwetok would later be the site of U.S. A-Bomb and H-Bomb tests from 1947 to 1952.

Our next stop was Saipan, the largest island of the Northern Marianas, which the Americans also captured from the Japanese in 1944. That's where our cargo was bound and where I would spend the next few weeks.

There were plenty of remnants of the great battle of Saipan—blown-up tanks, landing craft, and buildings. We tied up to a floating dock built by the engineers.

The island was "secure." That meant the battle was over except for some Japanese soldiers still hiding in the hills. A few at a time were being captured. They were kept in what looked like a horse coral. With no place to sit, they just squatted and looked scared. Saipan had been turned into a giant airfield for the B-29s that were bombing Japan.

The B-29 was a beautiful airplane, big and shiny and graceful. And the island was a very busy place with planes taking off and landing all the time. Trucks and building equipment were everywhere, and so were the navy and the marines.

I asked one Marine why so many guys were walking along the beach all hunched over. He told me they were looking for cat eyes. What the hell are cat eyes? I asked. He said they were semi-precious stones that sometimes washed up on the beach. Cat eyes are very pretty when polished and are used in making expensive jewelry, which these guys were doing. They were also making watchbands and bracelets out of aluminum from torn-up planes. They never ran out of material.

We were told that a Merchant Seamen's Club had just opened down the road. A few friends and I walked down the beach to the club, past a lot of wreckage from the invasion. The "club" turned out to be a former Japanese radio shack—three standing walls and a small part of the roof. We were given free cigarettes, stationery, and warm beer. We could have had cold beer on the ship, but it was an interesting walk. I'm glad someone told us not to walk in the area with the red flags stuck in the ground. Those were mines.

With the war in Europe over, the military devised a system of points to let people on the ship with the most service go home early. Many of these poor guys had been gone for years and had more than enough points to go home, but they hadn't been released and were not happy about it.

After our ship was finally unloaded in Saipan we zigzagged back to San Francisco. When we were about two days out we realized we had a stowaway on board. It turned out to be a Marine who wanted to go home. He was hiding in one of the holds and would sneak out in the middle of the night to grab some of the night lunch left out for the crew. He was spotted several times but no one reported him.

Our trip back to California was uneventful even though there were submarines lurking in the Marianas. We learned later that one of them sank the cruiser *Indianapolis* after it delivered the atomic bomb to Tinian.

As the ship sailed into San Francisco Bay on July 27, 1945, you hardly realized there was a city there. Then, when you got to the bridge, San Francisco appeared like magic. Unlike the last time I went under the Golden Gate Bridge, this time I was happy. It's one of my favorite memories.

We anchored in the harbor. The first boat out to meet us was an MP boat. The captain called out the stowaway and turned him over. I guess the captain knew he was there all the time but didn't bother to lock him up on the ship. I often wonder what happened to that stowaway. He looked like he had gone through a lot of the war. I felt sorry for him.

We docked later in the day, two months and two days after we had left. A couple of days later I signed off the ship, got paid, and took a train to Chicago. I was now an old salt. I hadn't been home for several months and was really looking forward to going there.

For two weeks with nothing to do but play, I made the best of it. I did the Billy Goat, the College Inn at the Sherman Hotel, the Chicago and Oriental Theatres, and all the neighborhood places. Most of my friends were in uniform, and some were home on furlough. We had a ball.

(l-r) Unidentified soldiers, Billy Goat Sianis, "Boston" and GK at the original Billy Goat Inn, 1855 West Madison St., Chicago, 1945

One of my high school friends, Cliff Hall, had also joined the Merchant Marines and, luckily, he was in town. So when it was time to ship out we decided we would try to get on a ship together. We both liked New York, so we took the New York Central to the big city.

While we were on the train—August 15, 1945—we got word that the Japanese had surrendered, six days after the U.S. had dropped atomic bombs on Hiroshima and Nagasaki.

The war was over! Suddenly there was cheering on the train and a lot of booze appeared. It was a happy train that pulled into New York.

Cliff and I found a room at the Knickerbocker Hotel just off Times Square, where people were still celebrating in the streets. Our room was four dollars a night.

It wasn't much but it was better than the Jackson Hotel across the street for two-fifty a night. There, the rooms were too small to turn around in. Plus a lady would come around at night and ask if you wanted to be serviced. (I only know that because on a later trip I stayed there one night.) I preferred the Knickerbocker.

With the war over, suddenly everyone was happy. And now, when we signed on a ship we knew where it was going. Cliff and I went down to the National Maritime Union Hall on Tenth Avenue to look for one going to Europe.

The Union Hall was decorated with large photo murals of people fighting during the big strike in 1936 at the *SS California,* which led to Joseph Curran, the able-bodied seaman and boatswain who started the strike, to form the National Maritime Union in 1937, of which I was now a member.

A huge blackboard listed all the ships, where they were going and what jobs were available. We signed on to a Victory ship that was going to Le Havre, France.

A Victory ship is newer and larger than a Liberty ship and built to carry cargo. It's made to sit in the water, not on the water. When it's not loaded, it carries ballast to hold it down.

But after the war there was a shortage of troop ships, so many of the Victory ships were converted to troop carriers. When these ships were converted, the holds were filled with bunks, sometimes six high and without much ventilation. The weight of the troops was nowhere the weight of a normal cargo. This is not a fun way to cross the ocean.

We sailed to Le Havre without any problems. It was nice to sail in a straight line instead of zigzagging. When we got to France the ship needed some minor carpentry work which was done by German prisoners of war. I was surprised to see that some of them looked like they were 11 or 12 years old.

Le Havre was a sad place. The French were starting to put it back together after all the war damage, but they had a long way to go. Cliff and I took a couple of cartons of cigarettes, which were better than money, jumped on the back of an army truck and went to town. We did some drinking and carousing and went back to the ship. I didn't care much for Le Havre, though, and was glad to leave.

Westbrook
Victory,
*a cargo ship
converted to
a troop
transport,
on which
GK served in
1945*

The next day we started loading the happiest bunch of GIs I ever saw. Many of them had been scheduled to go to Japan for the invasion, but when the atomic bomb was dropped their orders changed. They were going home. Their debarkation camp was named Camp Lucky Strike. It's no wonder everyone smoked. All the K rations had cigarettes in them.

For some stupid reason, the GIs were paid before they got on the ship. With 10 or 12 days at sea and nothing to do, the Victory ship turned into a gambling ship. Everywhere you turned there was a card game or a crap game. Some of the guys did very well and some went broke.

We hit rough weather and the ship bounced around like a cork. It was hell sleeping below deck in those cargo holds. There were a lot of seasick soldiers. I think the lucky ones were the ones too seasick to gamble because they still had some money when they got to New York. Turned out there were more losers than winners on that trip.

It's hard to describe the experience of coming into New York Harbor on a troop ship after World War II. Many boats came out to greet us, fireboats shooting water into the sky, with hundreds of other boats and ships blowing their horns. The GIs were all over the ship, hanging on the ladders, climbing the masts, cheering at the top of their lungs as the ship played big band music over the P.A. Huge "welcome home" signs hung on buildings and storage tanks everywhere. What a sight!

Two days later Cliff and I signed off the ship and into the Knickerbocker Hotel. After a week in New York trying to see how fast we could spend our money, we were back in the Union Hall looking for another ship. We didn't want to go back to La Havre. We found two openings on another converted Victory ship going to Marseille and decided we'd give France another chance.

GK and shipmate, Floyd Bickel, 1946

It was a good choice. Marseille was a huge, exciting port. Many sunken ships were still in the harbor but the city seemed to be going full blast. I never saw so many different foreign soldiers speaking languages I had never heard.

We had plenty of cigarettes so we could do the town. Because there was limited dock space we had to anchor out for a few days and that gave us more time ashore. Everywhere guys were selling black market stuff.

We bought Chanel No. 5 perfume, gold jewelry and watches. I bought a "gold" pocket watch. When it stopped working I opened it up and found one big spring in it, period. It worked for about an hour. We found out later all of it was counterfeit. I have to give those crooks credit. They were really sharp operators.

There was a lot of drinking going on. We easily made friends with the GIs who wanted to hear all about the States. One night, after drinking with them very late

at the Pink Elephant, we went outside, where one of the GIs insisted on giving us his jeep. He said he wouldn't need it anymore. While Cliff and I were discussing what we would do with the jeep, several MPs showed up to take him away.

I remember the chief MP was a major with a big chrome revolver. We insisted we should go with the soldier because he was our friend. The major took one look at us and said, "OK, you guys wait on the corner here and I'll come back for you." Thank God, he never did. I hope that poor GI didn't get in too much trouble.

We never took the jeep either, but it was late and there were no water taxis running. In order to get back to our ship anchored in the harbor, we hired a man with a row boat. There were several Victory ships at anchor and they all looked alike. The man had to row to four or five ships before we found the right one. He kept complaining so we kept giving him more cigarettes.

Finally our ship was loaded with another group of happy GIs. The weather was beautiful in the Mediterranean. We told the soldiers to stay awake so they could see the Prudential sign on the Rock of Gibraltar (from Prudential's ad slogan "Get a piece of the Rock"). Some of them believed us. Once again, the ship turned into a gambling ship.

When we got into the North Atlantic and into rough weather there were a lot of seasick guys but who were still very happy to be going home. We would often pass the *Queen Mary* and *Queen Elizabeth* in the middle of the ocean. Painted battleship gray, the Queens were also used as troop ships, but they were huge and a lot more stable than our Victory ship. Everyone would rather be on one of those, especially in a storm.

Back in New York, Cliff and I checked into the Knickerbocker again. We decided to have a little fun before signing on another ship. But money didn't go far in New York and we soon found ourselves in need.

Months earlier in Chicago I had taken a picture of my girlfriend, Beverly Nicolas, shooting pool at her father's pool table in their basement. The wall next to the table was covered with pictures of Petty Girls cut out from *Esquire* magazine. The picture of her shooting pool had the pin-up pictures in the background. It was a nice shot.

Just before joining the Merchant Marines, I sent this and some other pictures to several magazines but never heard back. I forgot about them until a friend said he saw Bev's photo in the overseas edition of *Look Magazine*. A full page. The caption was, "See what the boys are fighting for?"

I said to Cliff, "Let's go over to *Look Magazine*. I think they owe me some money." We told a woman in the editorial office the story. After a short wait, she came back and handed me a check for $50. We were good for a few more days ashore, and then it was back to Union Hall to look for another ship.

We found two openings on a former luxury liner called the *John Ericsson,* scheduled to leave April 4, 1946, for England to pick up a shipment of war brides. We had never been to England and thought it would be a good change of ship and scenery.

The ship docked in Southhampton and we had enough time off to go to London. On the train into the city, we passed one airfield after another. I really liked London. Though there was plenty of damage from the bombings, everyone was in high spirits because the war was over. And though some nightclubs were for members only, the good part was that you could join at the door. Cliff and I joined many clubs that night. Everyone was glad to see us and it was easy to make friends. The natives spoke English.

Back at the ship the war brides came on board and we took off for New York. Since the weather was good and it was a large ship, there weren't as many seasick passengers.

We had very little access to the war brides who were guarded by armed soldiers. One of the guards told me they were guarding government property. Some of the women had babies. I felt very sorry for one of them. She had a black baby and asked me what kind of state Alabama was. I told her it was warm. I hope she made out OK.

After that trip, Cliff and I went back to Chicago for some serious R&R.

GK photo ID for Buenos Aires, Argentina shore leave, 1947

CHAPTER THREE

The Long Voyage Home

I always knew during R&R it would be time to ship out again soon. Though the wars in Europe and Japan were officially over, the draft was still on to build forces for the armies of occupation and I was still fulfilling my service with the Merchant Marines. Cliff wanted to get a ship from New York but I'd heard that Australia was a fantastic place with beautiful, over-sexed girls, so we split up. I ran into Richard Donafsky, another friend from high school who had joined the Merchant Marines and was ready to ship out too. He agreed that Australia sounded great.

So we decided to hitchhike to California to get a ship. After five short lifts, two in the back of pick-up trucks, we hadn't even gotten to St. Louis and were pretty discouraged. Then the good luck kicked in. Our next lift was a young guy in a beautiful green 1941 Chevy coupe. He was delivering the car to Los Angeles for a dealer and wanted company. There is a God.

We took Route 66 and like the song says, all the way to Los Angeles we had many kicks. We even talked our new friend into taking a side trip to Douglas, Arizona, so we could walk across the border into Agua Prieta, Mexico, to buy some souvenirs. It was a dusty little town then but I understand 77,000 plus people live there today.

Back on Route 66 we stopped at Tombstone, Arizona. In those days, there weren't any tourists, but luckily we ran into an old man who looked like he'd just stepped out of a cowboy movie. He showed us the town, Boot Hill Cemetery, the Birdcage saloon, and told us stories about Geronimo hiding back there in the hills.

Salome Where She Danced, Arizona, 1946 (Photo by Richard Donafsky)

Another stop was Salome Where She Danced, Arizona, a town named by humorist Dick Wick Hall, after he watched the wife of the town's founder, Salome Pratt, try to walk on the hot desert sand in her bare feet and proceeded to "dance" to her destination. (No relation to the Biblical Salome.) When we were there, it was practically a ghost town. I know these places today are probably overrun with tourists but I don't want to go back again. I'll keep my memories intact.

When we got to Los Angeles our friend dropped us off near Union Station. It was late, so we went inside. We had just settled down to sleep in the great, soft leather chairs when a cop asked us to leave.

So we went on to San Pedro, where we would look for a ship. We arrived very late and decided to sleep on a park bench. Soon, another cop came by and told us we should go sleep in the railroad station. You can't win.

The next day we checked into the Miramar Hotel. Near the Union Hall, it was far from first-class but it was cheap and where a lot of seamen stayed between trips. Down the street was Shanghai Red's tavern, a rough, tough hangout of old salts who loved to drink and fight. I was afraid to go in the place.

Richard Donafsky and GK hitchhike to California, 1946

Every morning we went to the Union Hall and sat around waiting for a ship to Australia. After a week, as seamen say, "on the beach," Donafsky gave up and took the first ship he could get. I decided to wait a little longer. I really wanted to go to Australia. But after another week I had to give up, too. I'd sold anything I had of value and had even gotten money from the Seamen's Welfare. It was time to get a ship not going to Australia.

The next day a ship was listed that needed an OS (Ordinary Seaman). It was to go through the Panama Canal, then to Brazil, and then back to New York. That was a good deal, because when I got off the ship in New York I would be paid $125 for transportation back to San Pedro. Of course, I would stay and ship out from New York.

I got the papers from the union and went over to sign on to the *Peter V. Daniel*, a name I'll never forget. It was a shabby Liberty ship that had seen better days. I thought, "Well, it wouldn't be a long trip and I always wanted to go through the Panama Canal." I hoped the crew would be easy to get along with.

Again, I lucked out. The crew was from central casting, with only two alcoholics and one drug addict. When we got to know each other we got along very well.

Here's a brief description of some of the guys I worked with and hung out with on the *Peter V. Daniel*. But first, I must tell you that, on a ship, most guys go by a nickname or by the job they do. The boatswain, the foreman of the deck crew, for example, is called Boats. That's why I don't remember or didn't even know many of their last names. With some, I never knew their first names. Anyway, meet the unforgettable crew.

Scotty and GK aboard the Peter V. Daniel, *1946*

Scotty, A.B. He was on my watch, so I saw a lot of him. In fact, we lived in the same cabin. He was probably in his late 70s, a small Scotsman who looked like Mahatma Gandhi. He had sailed clipper ships around Cape Horn and was full of sea stories.

Bill Hoe, A.B., around 40. He was the other man on my watch. Bill was half Swedish and half Mexican. He was small, like many Mexicans, but had the features of a Swede. He was from California and in the '30s had worked on the yacht of Preston Sturges, the famous movie director. He told great stories about Hollywood parties held on it. Humphrey Bogart anchored his large sailing yacht near the Sturges yacht. Bill said you could always tell when Bogart and his first wife were aboard because you could hear them fighting and throwing things, waking up the whole harbor.

Floyd Bickel, A.B., late 20s. He was my best friend on the ship, a tall, good-looking guy with a Clark Gable mustache. He was originally from Nebraska but had worked in Alaska before going to sea. He was a drinker, gambler, and carouser. A great role model. I don't know what we had in common but we hit it off immediately and when in port always went ashore together to see the sights.

(l-r) Floyd, GK, and Vic, 1946

Curley Soward, oiler, early 20s. Curley was my second best friend. He was in the Black Gang. That doesn't mean you're black. It means you work in the engine room. There are three departments on a ship—deck, engine and stewards.

I usually hung out with the guys in the deck department, but Curley and I had a lot in common. He was about my age and we got along well. A good ole boy from Texas who liked country music, he was always trying to get the *"Grand Ole Opry"* on his Hallicrafters S-38 shortwave radio. We would listen for hours to shortwave radio programs from around the world.

Victorio, A.B., mid-20s. Vic was from California, a big, husky, six-foot, sweet-tempered Mexican who was good to have as a friend. I think he could break you in half if he felt like it but he was a really fun guy.

One day, my friend Bill told me to tell Vic he was a greaser. I wasn't up on West Coast ethnic slurs and thought he said geaser. So I said to Vic, "I hear you're a geaser." He said, "You mean greaser? Did Bill tell you to say that?" I said, "Yeah." He laughed and said, "Go tell Bill he's an asshole." I learned that greaser was a word you don't say to Mexicans. Thank God, Vic had a sense of humor.

Chuck, A.B., mid-20s. Chuck was another nice guy from California,—clean-cut, blond, and curly-headed—who looked like an ad for surfers. His life was cars. All he talked about was hot rods and the wonderful one he built back home.

Tex Samson, A.B., about 50. Guess what? He was from Texas. Tex liked to show you the scars on his ankles that he got from the shackles he wore when he was in a chain gang building a highway down South. He would drink anything he thought had alcohol in it. My favorite memory is Tex returning to the ship one night after a drinking binge in Genoa. He was coming up the gangway backwards while fighting off the octopus he said was chasing him.

"Poop Deck" and GK, 1946

Poop Deck, O.S., wiper, about 18. A wiper works in the engine room. Poop Deck was from Texas. He reminded me of a young Ross Perot: thin, short, high-pitched voice, feisty, and known for saying, "By god, I don't take crap from no one. I can lick my weight in wild cats!" He was a lot of fun.

Deck was the deck engineer, about 50. The deck engineer's job is to take care of the cargo winches and other machinery on deck. Right away you could tell Deck was from Ireland and had many hard miles on him. Years before, he had lost his false teeth and never replaced them but he could eat everything including apples and steak. Talk about hard gums!

Boats, the boatswain, about 60. The boatswain is in charge of the deck crew. He doesn't stand a watch; he just makes sure everyone on deck does his job. Boats was an old salt from Macedonia. Easy to get along with, all he wanted to do was talk politics and about the days before there was a maritime union.

The captain was Lewis E. Thomas. He was about 50, medium height, good-looking, with black hair and mustache. He reminded me of Jack Holt, the movie star that most of you wouldn't remember. I don't know where he was from but sometimes he had an English accent.

He was a hard drinker and often wouldn't leave his cabin for days. When he did, he would remind us that he was "the mah-ster of this vessel!" And sometimes he would come down and get in the crew's poker game that went around the clock when we were at sea. He wasn't a bad guy.

Then there was me. George. Soogie, O.S. I'll explain. On one ship they called me "Red," on another, "Whitey," and on another (my favorite), "Slim." On this ship I was called "Soogie."

On shore, when you wash down your walls you say you are washing down your walls. But when you do the same job on a ship, you are "sooging" the bulkheads. The union newspaper ran a comic strip called *"Soogie,"* a kind of seagoing Beetle Bailey. Somehow, I got identified with the main character that was always into something. Even the captain called me Soogie.

A week after I signed on, the cargo was loaded and we sailed out of San Pedro Harbor bound for Brazil via the Panama Canal.

The trip to Panama was pleasant. We had good weather, the work wasn't hard, and best of all I realized we had a great chief cook. I felt like a tourist. When we reached Panama we had to anchor for a day and wait our turn to go through the Canal. Then we picked up a pilot and started through the first set of three locks. It was exciting to see those huge gates open.

We had thrown our lines to workers on shore who tied them to electric cars, called "mules," that then pulled us slowly through the locks. It was an efficient and awesome operation. I think everyone should go through the Panama Canal, at least once in life.

After we went through the first set of locks, we crossed Gatun Lake to get to the next three locks. I was getting an education. I'd never known there was a large lake between the locks. After passing through the next set of locks we were in the Atlantic Ocean, headed south across the equator to Salvador, Brazil.

We made a short stop at Curacao, a Dutch island in what is now called the Netherlands Antilles, off the coast of Venezuela, and famous for Curacao liquor. It was an unusual place because the buildings were mostly of Dutch architecture, and for a tropical island to look like Holland was surprising. Another surprise came when a kid about nine or 10 came aboard the ship one day selling newspapers and souvenirs and speaking excellent English. I asked him how he did that. He told me the schools in Curacao teach the children two languages, Dutch and English.

At the entrance to the harbor a huge turntable bridge opened to let ships in, and then closed so traffic could go across the harbor. But late at night, the bridge was left open for ships to come in or out, stranding people on one side of the harbor or the other. If you were stuck on the side where all the bars and nightclubs were and you stayed too late, you'd have to hire a rowboat to row you back to the side where the ship was. How do I know this? I'm sure you can figure it out. Soon after the crew stocked up on the famous Curacao liquor, we were off to Salvador, Brazil.

Most ships hold a King Neptune ceremony when someone on board crosses the equator for the first time but everyone on this ship had done it before. We couldn't talk anyone into looking for the square bubbles on the equator.

Salvador is built on a bluff overlooking the harbor. Streetcars built on the same angle as the bluff take you up to the city. I'd never seen so many different kinds of people in one small city. People from all over the world mingled with Brazilian Indians from the backwoods.

The highlight of the trip was the night a half dozen of us went to a nightclub that looked like a poor man's Rick's Café in the movie *Casablanca*. The nightclub featured a band and a floorshow and we were there quite a while. When it was time to leave we couldn't find a waiter, so we decided to just walk out figuring somebody would run after us with the check.

But it wasn't until we were out on the street that we were stopped. By the police! We quickly paid the tab with a big tip and returned to the ship. We were in Salvador only two days. I would have liked to stay longer and seen more.

The next day we were off on the short trip to Santos, Brazil, where the major portion of our cargo would be unloaded. There was no room at the dock when we arrived so we had to anchor in the harbor for a few days.

These were the days before container ships, which are loaded and unloaded in a couple of days. It could take weeks for the old style freighters to load or unload a ship, so when we finally got to the dock we knew we would be there for at least two weeks.

On the beach,
Santos, Brazil, 1946

I liked Santos. It is a major seaport with wonderful beaches, hotels, nightclubs and many small waterfront bars with some of the best Brazilian music I ever heard. I had my first "gin tonica" in Santos. We call it gin and tonic, but it wasn't yet popular in the States. Brazilian tonic had a lot of quinine in it to fight malaria. I sure didn't want to get malaria, so I did my best to fight it off with gin tonicas.

When a ship is in port you don't stand watches. You work days like you would ashore, painting and keeping everything shipshape, and you have the nights off. Floyd and I had plenty to explore in Santos. We often took the No.15 streetcar from the docks to the other side of town with its modern movie theater, a beautiful beach, and a gorgeous hotel whose name I don't remember. Floyd and I spent a couple of weekends at the Hotel Atlantico, a lesser hotel on the beach but across the street from the gorgeous no-name hotel.

No-name had an outdoor nightclub like nothing I had ever seen. The white, translucent dance floor was lit from beneath, making the dancers appear to float in the air. There were colored lights in the huge trees. The tables were glass, also with lights beneath and flowers that grew up through their centers. The hotel's great orchestra played Latin and American music. The only time I saw or heard anything similar was years later in Havana, Cuba.

Floyd and I never went in. I don't think we would have been welcome. Everyone there was dressed in formal clothes. So we just watched through the trees.

One weekend we decided to visit São Paulo, a large city up in the mountains. The bus ride from Santos took us through miles of banana plantations and little villages. Then we started to climb. São Paulo is 2,700 feet high. Because a new highway was in the process of being built, some of the ride was fine and some was very scary.

Many years later when I was photographing a big-time banker in Chicago from São Paulo, I told him about the time I came up the new highway when it was being built. He laughed and told me they had just finished the *second* super-highway.

When I was there, São Paulo had a population of about three million. Today it is one of the largest cities in the world with a population of over 20 million. São Paulo was major and interesting but I liked Santos better because it was less congested and easier to get around in. Plus the ship was there and handy to sleep in.

The best thing about being on a freighter is that you have just enough time ashore to wear yourself out and drain your batteries. Then you are back at sea with fresh air, good food, getting recharged and ready for the next port.

When you sign on a ship they tell you where you are going and when you will return. However, there is small print in the ship's articles that can change that, namely, an act of God. In other words, the shipping company, under certain conditions, can change the schedule.

So when, just before sailing, we were notified that our ship full of cotton and coffee was not going to New York but to Barcelona, Spain, and Genoa, Italy, I thought, what the hell? There was nothing I could do about it and I did want to see some of Spain and Italy.

On the way, we stopped for a day at Gibraltar, where there clearly had been a lot of aerial bombing. You could still see partially sunk ships throughout the harbor. Once we'd anchored, a couple of "bum boats" rowed spookily out of a large hole in the hull of one of those half-sunken ships. They were called bum boats because they were loaded with souvenirs and other stuff they tried to sell to crews of newly arrived ships. I don't know why we stopped at Gibraltar because we never got to the dock. But we did buy stuff from the bum boats.

When we arrived in Barcelona, I don't think an American ship had been there in a long time. Most of the people seemed sad but they smiled when they learned we were Americans and were glad to see us. One bartender said, "I have something special for you." From a back shelf he pulled out an old bottle, with a faded label, of American bourbon. It wasn't our drink of choice, but we had some anyway because he was so pleasant.

In spite of the sadness and the extremes we saw, Barcelona was beautiful. At night, people dressed to the hilt, drove around in Rolls Royces and other fine cars, but back at the ship, we'd see threadbare poor people digging in the ship's garbage. There didn't seem to be much of a middle-class.

After several days of unloading the cotton, we were off to Genoa with the coffee. When we tied up, there was sudden confusion about the cargo. It seems a lot of coffee was missing. I don't know the facts, but I thought I saw a couple of truck loads of coffee leave the ship with the cotton in Barcelona. Although one of our mess men was arrested going through the security gates with a bag of coffee under his coat, he was later let go. It would take a hundred years to steal the amount of coffee missing, one little bag at a time.

Genoa seemed to be recovering well from the war. Our first night ashore Floyd and I checked out the available entertainment. The Golden Beetle was a very welcoming club, and there were many smaller bars just as friendly.

I remember one in particular where a lot of British seamen hung out. Whenever the drinking got heavy and they started singing *"Somewhere Over the Rainbow"* you knew a fight was about to break out. But the owner had a big German Shepherd that acted as a bouncer. When the dog came out, the fighting stopped.

The best place in Genoa was the Scandinavian Club. It was a genuine nightclub with a huge dance floor and a large band which did live radio broadcasts. I don't think the station was very powerful but the whole setup was very civilized.

I had bought a bolt of genuine 100 percent British wool from one of the bum boats in Gibraltar. I thought Genoa would be a good place for a real Italian tailor to make me a suit. I found a little shop and a tailor who said he could make a suit in a couple of days.

He spoke English well and told me he had lived in Brooklyn, New York, for several years but got homesick and came back to Italy before the war. He praised Mussolini for, among other things, making the trains run on time. He also said most Italians still liked Mussolini and were sorry for the way he ended.

I liked the tailor. He made me a fine brown pinstriped suit from the material I bought. But it wasn't long before I realized that material wasn't 100 percent British wool. I was screwed. If you looked at it wrong, it wrinkled. Wearing it for a day made it look slept-in for a week. Plus I looked like a gangster in that suit. It was just as well. With cigarettes going for 50 cents a carton on the ship, it was no great financial loss. I sold the suit to an Italian guy very cheap.

One night I came back to the ship and there were a half-dozen American soldiers eating in our mess hall. Turned out they were a special detached police unit looking for a stolen train. Can you believe someone had stolen a whole train?

When the trail of the stolen train led them to Genoa, the soldiers looked for an American ship because they knew the food would be good. The captain told the cook to feed them. After a good meal they thanked the captain and left to look for the train. I wonder if they ever found it.

Another night I came back to the ship and an Italian family was in our mess hall eating beautiful filets mignon. I asked the cook what was going on. He said he was told to feed the family while the captain entertained their daughter in his cabin. What a ship.

The crew was about worn-out from Genoa. It was time to go back to sea, get recharged and be on our way home at last. Then the word came down. We were not going to New York but back to Santos, Brazil. What the hell was going on? What happened to my six-week voyage? Floyd said they must have gotten another contract for cotton and coffee. He also reminded me that they couldn't keep us out for more than a year.

So a couple of days later we were on our way back to Santos. I liked Santos, but I wondered when this trip would end. On the way to Santos we stopped at Las Palmas, Canary Islands for two days to drop off some small stuff. You could buy a canary there in a handmade cage, but I didn't need a canary.

With just two days, we didn't have time to see much of Las Palmas. It turned out, however, that one of our crew, a wiper named Domingos, was a refugee from the Canary Islands. If he went ashore, he'd be arrested. A couple of army soldiers guarded the gangway the whole time we were in port, ready to grab him if he tried. But he didn't try.

Domingos's family was still in Las Palmas. Each day, they came down to the ship to see him but they couldn't come aboard either. It was sad to see them talking to each other yet not be able to get together.

Transferring a stowaway, 1946

When we were leaving and they came down to wave goodbye to him, the captain let Domingos stand on the bridge so he'd look like he was running the ship and impress his family. The captain wasn't a bad guy. Plus being captain wasn't the easiest job in the world. Once, in the middle of the Atlantic ocean we found a stowaway. The captain wired a passing ship going back to the stowaway's home port and six of us and the first mate put the stowaway in a lifeboat and rowed him to the ship. We sent him back home, right in the middle of the ocean, by order of the captain.

It was good to get back to Santos. We had spent almost a month there before, knew our way around, and had made a few friends. This time we were tied up next to a banana boat. It was no problem to walk over to the boat and help ourselves to bananas. Everyone in the crew had plenty. Even the chief steward took a lot and I'm sure he charged the shipping company for them, too. I didn't know you could eat bananas in so many forms. We had them fried, in soup, in salads, in cakes, in pies, and more. It was a long time before I could look at another banana.

I don't want to give the impression that when in port all you do is play. You still have to do a full day's work on the ship. The stevedores do all the loading and un-loading, but the crew has plenty to do to keep everything running smoothly. And, of course, there is always chipping and painting. But there was still time for fun.

The ship was nearly loaded when the word came down that we were going back to Italy. Venice. I looked at Floyd and said, "Jesus Christ, we're on a goddamn tramp steamer."

Floyd agreed. It felt like Gilligan's Island. Going on a short cruise that never ends. Floyd said, "What the hell, they can't keep us out over a year and Venice is supposed to be a great place."

So a few days later we said goodbye to good old Santos and headed north for Venice, via the Atlantic Ocean and into the Mediterranean Sea through the Straits of Gibraltar. I always liked to go through the Straits at night because I could see the lights twinkling on the North Africa side. I imagined all kinds of exotic things going on and wished I was there.

One night I was lookout on the bow. It was pitch dark and I could see nothing. Suddenly, a light appeared directly in front of the ship. I frantically called the bridge and we changed course to miss it. The mate told me it was a fishing boat. The fishermen didn't have electricity, so they used oil lamps for navigation. Oil was expensive so they wouldn't light the lamps unless they thought they'd be run down by a big ship. I'm glad I was awake.

I don't remember why we made a brief stop at Brindisi, a small city in southern Italy but I remember that I ate my first and best pizza there. It was in a little restaurant that had to be 200 years old, with a clay oven and plenty of atmosphere. I went back the next day and had an enormous submarine sandwich. I sat outside on the patio under an umbrella eating this sandwich. A couple of crew members walked by on their way to look over the town and when they came back over an hour later I was still eating the sandwich. The wine was good, too. I didn't get to see much of Brindisi, but that's OK. The food made up for it.

The next day we headed up the Adriatic Sea to Venice. We were lucky to get a berth at the end of the Grand Canal. Most people don't realize what a large industrial city Venice is. Because we were docked at the end of the Grand Canal we would be able to take the water bus to the Piazza San Marco or, as we say, Marco Square, the heart of Venice.

As soon as we could, Floyd and I headed to Marco Square to check it out. I had seen pictures of Venice, but they didn't come close to actually being there. Like Genoa, Venice was recovering pretty well from the war. The narrow side streets with small shops and restaurants were interesting but nothing compared with Marco Square. The Basilica, the Doge's Palace, the Bell Tower, and the great open piazza looked like a movie set.

We were standing in front of the Doge's Palace when a man came up to us and offered to give us a private tour for two packs of cigarettes. He said next year the tourists would start coming

GK at San Marco Square,
Venice, Italy, 1946

back and he would make lots of money, but, for now, he would settle for the cigarettes. It was still early afternoon. We had all day and night to see Venice so we invested in the two packs. It was one of our best investments.

At the time I didn't even know what a Doge was. We saw every nook and cranny of the palace, and our guide told stories to go with each one. I especially liked the courtroom of the Council of the Terrible Ten. If a person were found guilty, he would be led through a door, across the Bridge of Sighs to the prison. The prison had one room for strangling a prisoner, another for chopping his head off, and other rooms for other tortures. Our guide showed us the sword used for head chopping. It was worn down in the middle. Those people sure believed in swift justice. But in spite of that, needless to say, we thought Venice was spectacular.

One day, though, I had a bad toothache. The captain sent me to a local dentist the shipping company used. His office was on the third floor of an old building overlooking a small plaza. It wasn't very modern. The dentist operated the drill with a foot pedal, like a sewing machine.

While I was in the chair, he pointed out a pile of rubble on the other side of the plaza. "Before the war I had a modern office in that building. The Americans bombed it." I almost jumped out of the chair and ran out of the office, but the tooth hurt so much I decided to take a chance. The dentist ended up pulling it and not killing me. Actually, he was very nice to me and did a good job on my tooth. He knew I didn't bomb his office.

After a couple of weeks we were ready to sail again. We had been away from the States so long we were running low on some supplies. But Italy wasn't the best place to stock up a ship. There were still many shortages because of the war.

The chief cook watched the loading of supplies. He said one funny-looking side of beef looked more like camel. He was a great cook, and he wasn't happy when he found out where we were going next. We would make a short stop at Split, Yugoslavia, where no supplies were available, and then south to Argentina.

The chief cook knew his job so well that when he made cracks about running out of food we took him seriously. But the chief steward said, "There's no way that could happen. I'll put my money on the cook." So the ship was loaded and we made the short trip to Split to drop off a small amount of cargo.

Split is a city in Croatia, my father's homeland, so I was really looking forward to seeing some of Croatia (which was then part of Yugoslavia). But after the news that we were going to Argentina, I told Floyd, "I give up. I'll quit bitching. We'll get to New York eventually. As the saying goes, I might as well lie down and enjoy it."

The Italian side of the Adriatic Sea is rather plain, but the Yugoslavian side is beautiful with many large and small islands, some with palm trees and snow-capped mountains in the background. And though there is great natural beauty, Split was in bad shape. During the war, first the Germans bombed it and then the Americans bombed it. There was a lot of rebuilding to do, but it was easy to see that in better days Split was a beautiful city dating back to the Roman days.

The unloading of the cargo was unusual. Split was the only port we visited that didn't use trucks to unload. They used horses and wagons. It was like watching an old movie, but they got the job done.

One night, Floyd and I walked ashore to a small hotel on the waterfront. There were several men sitting around a table in the lobby. I said hello in Croatian, one of about ten words I knew in the language. That got their attention. When I told them my father was from Croatia we immediately became friends. They insisted we share their Turkish coffee, which was thick like molasses and very sweet. We had a cup, but only one. We didn't like it, but we didn't want to hurt their feelings.

They spoke very good English. They told us some war stories and offered to show us around town and see the ancient Diocletian's Palace just a few blocks away. We declined and went back to the ship. You must remember I was still a teenager with not enough brains to take advantage of a good thing. I went to Split 50 years later and realized what I had missed.

On the way back to the ship we ran into a group of people rebuilding a cobblestone street that had been blown up. It seems that every night after work whole families would come and work on the reconstruction. Yugoslavia was a Communist country then. I don't know if the people were forced to do the work, but they didn't seem to mind.

Just before we sailed for Argentina a passenger came aboard, a tall, well-dressed man with a big mustache. To this day, I still wonder who he was. On the long trip to Argentina the only time I saw him was while I was on watch, late at night, when he walked around the ship. I never heard him speak and didn't even know what language that would be. He was spooky. A few years later I read about big-shot Nazis who fled to Argentina after the war. I bet he was one of them.

Now we were off on the long trip to the well-named city of Buenos Aires. Down the gorgeous Adriatic, across the Mediterranean, through the Straits of Gibraltar (at night), and across the equator again to the South Atlantic. The trip was uneventful until about ten days out from Buenos Aires.

The quality of food was dropping. We were running low on everything and eating a lot of pasta and canned goods. We had a meeting with the chief steward to find out what was going on. He said we wouldn't starve, but we had to make do with what we had. He said he had trouble in Italy getting what he wanted, but that there was plenty of good food in Argentina and he would stock up with the best.

The meeting ended with the promise that he would be thrown overboard if he didn't follow through. I think a couple of guys were serious.

There are three big walk-in refrigerators on the ship: one for meat, one for fish, and one for cheese. The day before we docked at Buenos Aires, we washed them and hosed them down because they were *empty*. But the steward kept his word. When we pulled up to the dock there were trucks waiting with the best of everything. Our great cook was smiling. That night, dinner was a feast.

To get to Buenos Aires, first you must travel several miles up the Platte River. At the mouth of the river is Montevideo, Uruguay. And that was a sight. Right there, the year before, the Nazis had scuttled their great warship the *Admiral Graf Spee* in neutral waters, to keep it from being sunk by allied navy ships lying in wait outside the mouth of the Platte. You could still see some of the superstructure of the huge ship jutting out of the water.

We sailed up the river past the yacht club and tied up in Buenos Aires. I could tell from the skyline it was a great city. But we had plenty of work to do on deck before we could go ashore.

While working and sweating on deck, a man came aboard to take a picture of each crew member for a visa which was necessary before we could go ashore. That picture is my favorite of all time. I look like Barnacle Bill's mean brother. *I* would be afraid of me.

After getting our work done, Floyd and I were ready to take on Buenos Aires. The first night was a night to remember. This great city had plenty of everything. And it was here I had my first real steak. My mother's idea of steak was to fry a thin piece of meat in a frying pan until it was well-done. I had never seen or tasted such a thick, juicy, tender steak like the one I had that first night in Argentina.

We hit some nightspots, and at one place I'm told I did the tango. On our way back to the ship we were a bit noisy. A cop stopped us and asked for I.D. He looked at my picture and then at me. He laughed and said, "Vamoose." Nice cop.

The next Saturday Floyd and I were both free for the whole day. My father had a friend in Buenos Aires and suggested I should look him up if I had a chance. Floyd and I were standing on a busy corner looking at a map trying to figure out if we were near my father's friend's house when a man in his late twenties came by and asked if he could help. He spoke perfect English, which was great. I don't think he was a native.

I showed him the address. He said it was quite a way out. We would have to take a couple of buses and we'd probably get lost. He asked what we were doing in town. He was glad to meet a couple of American seamen and invited us to have a drink with him.

He took us to a beautiful outdoor café nearby. After our drinks came, the waiter brought a large tray heaped with all kinds of sandwiches. I asked who ordered the sandwiches. The man said it's the custom here. They put all those sandwiches in front of you. If you eat any you are charged, if you don't, there's no charge. We ended up having lunch.

Afterward, the man said that he had nothing to do that day and would be happy to show us around town. Why not? Floyd and I were both wondering what the catch was, but we didn't say anything.

We ended up having a tremendous time seeing the city and got along really well with our new friend. He suggested we have dinner, and that sounded good too. But first, he wanted us to stop at his apartment to drop something off.

We figured this is it: he's got some evil plan in mind. What the hell, we thought, there are two of us and we're both bigger than he is. We'll take a chance.

His apartment was nice but nothing special. He said he had just closed a business deal and was planning to go to the Andes for a vacation. He had been on his way from the bank when he met us and had some money he didn't want to walk around with at night. Then he pulled out this big wad of cash from his pocket, put it in a drawer and said, "OK, let's go out to dinner."

We couldn't believe it. He was just a nice guy. I wish I could remember his name and I wonder what his business deal was. He took us to another beautiful restaurant. While we were eating, a large crowd of people with torches came running down the street shouting in Spanish. They broke a few shop windows. I said, "What the hell is that?" He said, "It happens all the time. They're unhappy about something." Since the Perons were still in power I thought it might be political, but our friend didn't seem to want to discuss it.

We ate a great meal and later did some carousing. The evening was fun, we said goodbye, went back to the ship and never saw him again. I guess you could call meeting him was luck but it was the best part of our trip to Buenos Aires, a really spectacular city. I missed the wonderful food and music the minute we left.

The next morning Floyd woke me up with the news of where we were going next. New York, I hope? Not quite. Cape Town, South Africa! I couldn't believe it. I am truly on a tramp steamer. Well, I told myself, maybe I'll see a lion or an elephant.

A couple of days later, we left the dock and traveled back down the Platte River, past the *Graf Spee* and into the South Atlantic for the very long trip to Cape Town and what would be some startling revelations about how that city handled race problems.

I knew prejudice existed but I was unprepared for Cape Town. All my life I'd had black friends. And that summer in the Union Stock Yards the majority of my co-workers were black. We had fun fooling around and they liked to tease me. They called me Young Blood. (I was 16 years old.) I had one friend who looked like Joe Louis, only bigger. One of my jobs was to shovel cold ground meat into a chute that dropped to the floor below and into cans on a conveyor belt.

When the cans below started to come out half empty, my large friend appeared and said, "Move over, Young Blood." He kept the chute filled with no effort. That cold ground meat was really heavy. Soon after, I was transferred to canned hams.

Anyway, the Merchant Marines had been desegregated a long time before. (In my class at Maritime School we had a black guy named White. Also a white guy named Black.) And some of our crew were black. Though I had never been down south where there were separate water fountains for "Colored" and "White," I was really shocked at Cape Town. No wonder they had a revolution.

We tied up at the edge of town. Princess Elizabeth of England had been there the week before and a long line of bleacher seats still stood along the road from the docks to the town. I guess Cape Town held quite a reception for her.

Blacks were doing the unloading and anything else that required manual labor but I noticed none of them used tools. A foreman told me they were forbidden to use even a hammer or a screwdriver. They weren't allowed to learn or do anything but hard labor. What a shame. Cape Town was not a happy place.

But it was a larger and more modern city than I expected. Cable cars went to the top of Table Mountain, but while we were there it was too windy to go up. It must have been a fantastic view.

We were there only a few days but every place we went—restaurants, movie theatres, bars, cabs—there were signs that said "Europeans Only." "But we're not Europeans. You let Americans in?" we'd ask sarcastically. I was glad to leave Cape Town.

So, where the hell did we go next? Can you believe, China, by way of Singapore? Would I ever see Chicago again? For now, all we had to do was round the Cape of Good Hope and cross the Indian Ocean. It became an interesting trip when we got near India.

Curley—my friend who worked in the engine room and who was on the same watch as mine—and I spent a lot of time together. We would sit up at night and pick up British radio dramas from India which they broadcast to their Forces overseas. The British announcers never said "Armed Forces," just "Forces." It was funny to hear them say "Welcome, Forces."

Many of the programs were very good. And unlike American radio, the British used swear words. How civilized to hear an actor call someone a bastard. I wish I had a picture of Curley and me having cocktails from our private stock, listening to British radio and sailing up the South China Sea. I felt so international.

It was really interesting when we neared land. We passed through the Strait of Malacca past Borneo to Singapore. We docked at a small island off the mainland. It was like a suburb. I don't know why we stopped there because it was just overnight.

I think the captain had some private deal going on. We were told not to leave the ship because we were sailing in the morning. Someone else, however, told us there was a big bar on top of a hill near where the ship was docked.

That night, after the captain went ashore, about six of us decided to check out the bar. If we walked around the back of the hill we wouldn't be seen going up there.

It was about a half-hour's walk up the hill, and I'll never forget it. We passed through a native village where I saw types of people I had never seen before: dark-skinned people with very fine features, Malaysians, other types of Asians, and some races I didn't recognize at all. They wore loincloths, sheets of some kind, and strange clothes. It was dark and spooky. I was scared.

We passed a hut. Hanging outside were what I thought were shrunken heads. They turned out to be faces carved out of coconuts. I was happy when we got to the top of the hill and walked into a great-looking bar with a pool table.

And sitting at a big table with some people was our captain. "What the hell are you doing here?" he roared. No answer. "Have one drink and get back to the god-damn ship!" It was a pleasant five-minute walk down the front of the hill back to the ship. The next morning we sailed for China.

Though we were scheduled to go to Shanghai, at the last minute we went to Tsing Tao instead, 300 miles north of Shanghai. I was disappointed. I had never heard of Tsing Tao. Turns out the city is famous for its beer. A German colony had built a brewery there in 1903 and had made really good beer since that time, so good the brewery is still operating today.

We docked close enough to the town that we could walk to it. It was a very busy city. Everyone seemed to be selling something. Because the U.S. Navy Seventh Fleet was stationed there, the town had many bars and souvenir shops, even a small department store.

The Navy invited us to watch movies on one of their battleships. At night they set up a big screen out on deck. That was a treat. One night, I was sitting next to a nervous sailor who told me he hoped he didn't get caught. I said, "What did you do?" He said he was wearing the wrong-colored socks. Now I knew why I had joined the Merchant Marines. Half the time I didn't wear any socks.

Shipmates ashore at Tsing Tao, China, 1947

Floyd and I hired a rickshaw and toured the town. That was a great experience. Most of the rickshaws were shabby and so were the drivers. You could tell who the few rich guys in town were. They had beautiful polished wooden rickshaws with shiny bright sidelights and a brass horn. Their drivers were perfectly dressed and at least six feet tall. You couldn't miss them. It was like having a Rolls Royce and chauffeur in any other place.

I bought many souvenirs, including a leather suitcase with a figure of a dragon embossed on it. The Chinese currency was massively inflated. For the smallest purchase you needed handsful of money.

The whole city was nervous because the Chinese army was close by and everyone seemed to know that it wouldn't be long before the Communists would come out of the hills and take over the city. I didn't want to be around then.

Tsing Tao beer was good, but they also sold very poor vodka in pop bottles with a cap like a coke bottle has. They called it vodka, but many people got sick on it so I stuck to the beer.

The harbor was full of Chinese junks. Not a single one had sails that weren't made of a mass of patches. I think I recognized some parts of lifeboat covers from our ship, the *Peter V. Daniel,* and some of their lines looked familiar too.

I was afraid to find out where we were going next. We were back in the Pacific Ocean, a long way from New York. Then the word came down. Praise the Lord, we were going back to San Pedro, California, where we started from. I wouldn't get my $125 dollars for transportation back to California from New York but at least I was going home.

It was a long, long voyage back to the States but we wouldn't have much to do workwise. We had been gone so long that most of our paint was gone, used up or sold. It was a happy day when we sailed out of the harbor, past the junks with the patchy sails. I still couldn't believe we were on our way home.

Once at sea, we got back into the routine of standing watch and doing maintenance. And there was one job that I hated that we still had supplies for. It's called sluicing, and it's done to preserve all the wire rigging on the ship.

The job entails getting a bucket containing a mixture of fish oil and graphite and going to the top of the mast in a bosun's chair. Then you slowly ride down the rigging and, with a rag you dip in the bucket, you wipe the wire. It's a dirty, smelly job. Why didn't someone sell the fish oil in China? Well, at least this would be the last time I had to do it.

One dark night, I was at the wheel, half asleep, and the 3rd mate was dozing. When you steer with a gyrocompass there is a little clicking sound every time you move the wheel a half a degree. This night I heard the clicking getting faster so I turned the wheel hard over to get back on course. By the time I realized I had turned the wrong way, the ship was turning faster and the clicking was getting faster. I decided it was easier to keep going around than to try to go back. So in the middle of the ocean, at night, I made a 360-degree turn. And nobody noticed.

There is such a thing as cabin fever. We were out so long I'm surprised we didn't get it sooner. About three weeks from San Pedro, people started complaining about the food, which was OK, and then getting testy with each other. Day by day it got worse. Some friends stopped talking to each other or started accusing each other of one dumb thing or another.

About a week out of San Pedro I was steering when the captain came on the bridge. He said to me, "Look at that crooked wake. What the hell are you doing, zigzagging?" I told him I was going straight but the strong cross-currents made the wake uneven, which was true. He said he didn't want me steering his vessel anymore. I should split the steering with Bill and Scotty. That's great. I steer his *goddamn* ship around the world and, all of a sudden, a week from home, I don't know how to steer. Bill and Scotty were mad at me and said I did it on purpose.

Many other crew members were really going at each other. One guy was warned not to go on the fantail at night. He might fall overboard.

The last day out the captain invited the deck crew to his cabin. He said we had had a great trip and he wanted to have a drink with us. He was a regular Jekyll and Hyde. He poured out drinks from one of his bottles of really good Spanish brandy, of which he had bought several cases in Barcelona. No one took a sip before he did, not out of politeness but out of fear he was going to poison us. We thanked him and went to get the ship ready for docking the next day.

We tied up at the exact same spot we had left almost a year before. We had been around the world to North, South, and Central America, Europe, Asia, Africa, and several islands. Everywhere but Australia. To this day I have never been to Australia. My strong desire to see Australia left me many, many years ago. I don't think I'll ever make it there.

It took a few days before we could sign off, but some of the crew who lived in California got to go home for the night. Chuck came back the next day with the hot rod he was always bragging about. It looked like a Model A Ford chassis with a great big engine on it. Two seats with no doors and no roof. It wasn't my cup of tea but he loved it.

It was time to get paid off. I don't know if they still have the same system now, but then the system was to be paid off in cash. No one could get his or her hands on your money. No lawyer, finance company, or ex-wife could put a lien on your pay. You got the cash. If you owed anyone they would have to chase you. I think that's the reason some guys go to sea.

Everyone was packed and ready to leave the day we got paid. When we left, the *Peter V. Daniel* was in pretty bad shape and I heard the shipping agent say they were sending her to the boneyard.

I got my money, I think it was less than $1,000, and said some goodbyes. Sadly, I never saw or heard from any of the crew again. I got a cab and went to the Western Union office to wire my money home before someone hit me on the head, which was known to happen. In fact, when the cabdriver asked, "Long trip?" I answered, "No. Just coastwise from Seattle."

I wired the money, caught a cab to Union Station, and caught the first train to Chicago. I had completed my service as a merchant seaman with the U.S. Merchant Marines. I was on my way home and back to taking pictures. I was happy.

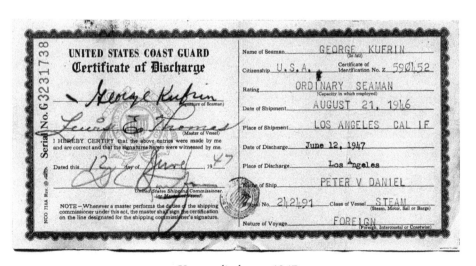

Voyage discharge, 1947

GK covers Sunbeam Corp. strike, Chicago, circa 1949
(Photo by one of the strikers)

CHAPTER FOUR

Freedom

I was glad to be back in Chicago. I spent the first few weeks relaxing and getting together with my friends. We were lucky not to have lost anyone close to us in the war, so it was like old times except for one big thing: we were all out of school and needed to find jobs. I knew I couldn't survive working for a couple of neighborhood newspapers. My mother always preached to me that there was nothing better than a steady job with a steady paycheck and a pension when you got old.

The place many Bohemians went for that kind of job was the Western Electric Company, sometimes called Bohemian U. It was located in a huge building covering several acres on the corner of Cermak Road and Cicero Avenue, the boundary line between the city of Chicago and the town of Cicero. When you cross over to the west side of Cicero Avenue, you are in Cicero. Al Capone's headquarters were once in the Hawthorne Hotel, located a block from Western Electric.

Bohemian U. factory was a great place to work if you wanted a steady job. Western Electric made the telephones, switchboards—in fact, all the equipment that had anything to do with telecommunications. Every year the company held a beauty contest so that employees could select their "Hello Charlie Girl," and this was a big deal. "Charlie" was the nickname for Western Electric employees.

During the summer, the entire factory shut down for a two-week vacation, and most of the employees got in their cars and traveled around the country. All of them were given a sticker photo of the year's "Hello Charlie Girl" to put on their car windshields. The idea was for company people to recognize other Western Electric workers when they ran into them around the country.

Many years later, when the factory became obsolete, there was serious talk of converting it into a prison, which is what the building looked like. The deal fell through, though, and eventually the factory was torn down.

I applied for a job at Western Electric. I'd heard if you were there for an interview during lunchtime, they gave you a free lunch, so that's when I applied. After filling out an application, a man took me into the factory and showed me the benches and what I'd be doing: twisting wire for switching equipment. I asked the man what the switch was for and he replied, "Some commercial building," and then told another employee that I was curious about what it was for. They hired me on the spot and said I could start that day. I stayed for the free lunch but I never went back.

I decided to try for another steady job and answered an ad in the neighborhood newspaper for a photographer at the Liquid Carbonic Co. This was an old company that made industrial gases, bottling equipment and custom-made soda fountains. Best of all, it was at Thirty-first and Kedzie, about a mile from my home. I got the job.

Liquid Carbonic had a huge photo studio run by two men, and also a great darkroom. Irwin Merry was the chief photographer, a very nice, heavy-set grey-haired old-timer, about 60, with a sense of humor. I liked him. His assistant, Bill Moraveck, a grumpy complainer in his late 40s, was the opposite of Mr. Merry. I got along with him but didn't care much for him. I always referred to myself as the third chief photographer. Bill didn't like that.

It was lucky I took the job because they had equipment I had never used. We shot almost everything with the 8x10 camera. (They called the 4x5 Speed Graphic the "miniature" camera.) I knew enough to carry my own weight, but I learned new techniques for lighting industrial machinery and material, mostly from Mr. Merry.

I was there only a few days when Bill said to take the miniature camera and go down to accounting and shoot photos for the company's house organ, which is what they used to call in-house magazines, of a woman who had just received a promotion. He gave me one holder (two sheets of film) and two flash bulbs.

When I came back quickly, Bill asked rather sarcastically, "Do you have to go back and do it over?" I told him one of the flash bulbs was defective and that instead of a flash I got a puff of smoke, but the other one was fine. "We'll see," he said. He developed the film and never said another word. They ran the picture big in the house organ.

After a few months the work began to get routine. It was fun at first to use the big cameras, but the novelty wore off when I realized I was getting into a rut. My favorite saying is, "The only difference between a rut and a grave is the depth." I looked around Liquid Carbonic and asked myself, "Is this where you want to be?"

I must say that just about everyone there was nice to me and I got along fine, but this place—like Western Electric—was not for me. I was there about six months, and the day they gave me a raise I quit. I almost felt guilty. A friend in the company's advertising department told me they couldn't believe what I just did. Nobody, but nobody, quits when they get a raise! That was my last steady payroll job. My mother was angry. But I felt as though I just got out of jail.

I went back to the neighborhood papers and weddings. The *West Side News* had folded and was replaced by the *Community Reporter,* a more professional group. They had me shooting some of the ads for advertisers. Every little bit helped, but I still wasn't getting rich.

It was time to pay a visit to my old friend, Vern Whaley, picture editor of the *Chicago Herald American.* He was glad to see me and helped me understand how the publicity picture business worked at that time. If you were a press agent and wanted to get a picture in the *Chicago Herald American* of some activity or person you were promoting, you would send a press release to the picture editor, Vern, and hope he would send a photographer to cover the event. Many times Vern would not have a photographer available, but if you sent him a picture he would try to run it.

If the press agent hired a photographer from Photo Ideas, which was Vern's publicity studio, you had a pretty good chance of getting your picture in the paper. I was certainly interested in working for him. He took me across the street to his small studio on the sixth floor of the Civic Opera House and introduced me to the man who ran it. He told the man to call me if he got bogged down.

As president of the Newspaper Guild, Vern also had another office down the hall. He used it to do the paperwork for the studio and also to handle the money. He always handled the money. He was quite an operator. Little by little, I got more and more work from him, especially if there was some major convention or trade show in town. Later on, when he was short a photographer at the paper, he would send me out on news assignments for the paper. That's how I met Gloria Swanson. There were several studios doing publicity pictures, but if you wanted to get in the *Chicago Herald American,* your best bet was to use Photo Ideas or INP.

The 10-story Hearst building on the corner of Madison Street and Wacker Drive housed three Hearst organizations: International News Service (INS), International News Photos (INP) and, on the second floor, the *Chicago Herald American*. The city room was right out of *"The Front Page"*—a big room full of reporters typing with two fingers, guys hollering on the phone, copy boys dashing around, no air conditioning, many fans, and the el train roaring by the open windows. It looked like total chaos but they got the paper out every day.

The night city editor was Harry Romanoff. He was short, heavy, and had a large, red nose. He looked like one of the seven dwarfs, but he had this fantastic voice. If you talked to him on the phone you would think you were talking to a movie star. He could get more news on the phone than most reporters got on the street. He would call a crime scene, ask for the person in charge, and get all the information by implying he was from "downtown." He was a master of the phone.

INS, the Hearst wire syndicate, was on the eighth floor. I didn't have much reason to spend time there. On the tenth floor was INP. Their logo was a Speed Graphic with wings on it.

You had to take the iron-caged elevator to the ninth floor and then walk up one floor to INP. You could bet on a horse, or a game, or anything else a bookie handles with the elevator operator on your way up.

The INP had what they called "sound photos," machines that could send pictures around the country. It worked like this. You put an 8x10 photo on a cylinder. On the other end a man would put a piece of 8x10 film on another cylinder. The first cylinder would turn and send light waves to the second one, exposing the film, which was then developed and, presto, they had the picture on the other end. The light was sent over phone lines. However, if there was any interference on the line during the transmission, some funny pictures came up, like heads shifted off the necks or feet next to the legs. They had a collection of funny transmissions.

The INP had a news department that serviced the country with news photos. They also had a commercial department that shot publicity pictures. Charlie "Nick" Nickels ran the news end; Don Alford ran the commercial department.

Nick was a man of medium height and weight. With his little mustache he looked like a relative of Ben Hecht. He was a very nice guy, quiet, always trying out a new lens. He would often come up to me and whisper the results of his tests. His job was to send and receive the sound photos. On occasion, he would hire a photographer to shoot features for one of the many Hearst magazines. I shot several for him.

One day he sent me to Comiskey Park to shoot a cover picture of Bob Feller for a Hearst sports magazine. I am not now or ever have been a baseball fan. When I got on the field before the game I had to ask, "Which one is Bob Feller?" They thought I was either joking or very stupid. The picture turned out OK, but I never felt at ease in a ballpark. Several years later Nick was running the photo department at Disneyland in California. When I took my family there, he got us free tickets for everything.

Don Alford was the complete opposite of Nick. He was about 60 years old, tall, thin, with a very loud voice, and he called everyone "sweetheart." Don was always talking about horses, hunting dogs, and guns. He could also tell stories about his early years when he would hire young pilots like Charles Lindbergh to fly film around the country.

Don was a great picture salesman. I met him through a couple of other photographers who did some work for him. One of his sales pitches was: "Use INP for your publicity picture and I'll try and put it on the wire." Although he was in competition with Vern's Photo Ideas, Vern still ran many of Don's pictures because

INP was also owned by Hearst. I was soon working for both of them. Vern had a full-time man running his studio, but Don used only freelancers. That meant he had more work for me.

Rudolph "Rudy" Seymour also did a lot of Don's work. He was a pear-shaped heavy-set guy in his late thirties. He was a lot of fun and very good at cheesecake and convention pictures. Because I was usually available, especially for last-minute shoots, I got more and more work, plus I was also working across the street for Vern.

Don liked for me to hang around. In case some shoot came up suddenly, I was right there to take the job. I soon found myself going downtown to the Hearst building almost every day. If Vern needed me, I was just across the street. It was working out well. Along the way I picked up some of my own clients. I worked out a deal with Don's darkroom man, Loren Kelley, to make prints for me.

It wasn't long before I had my own locker and use of a desk. The phone number on my business card was the same as INP. Don's secretary, Irene, would take calls for me when I wasn't there. I felt I had the best deal in town. I lost track of how many celebrities I photographed. Many were at the Palmer House.

Freddie Townsend, the P.R. man for the Palmer House, was Vern Whaley's best friend. Anything good that happened at the Palmer House appeared in the *Chicago Herald American*. I made many, many pictures there. One of my favorites was of Carol Channing when she appeared at the Empire Room of the Palmer House, the premier room in town.

At the time, I was also doing work for the Prudential Insurance Company of America. Prudential's ceo, Carroll Shanks, was in town and planning to have dinner at the Empire Room with his top people to see the Carol Channing show. Prudential had just divided its headquarters in Newark, New Jersey, into five regional home offices over which he was the boss. It was a big deal.

For the Chicago home office, the company had built Chicago's first skyscraper since the War, the Prudential Building. At 41 stories, it was not only the tallest building in Chicago but the sixth tallest in the world. When Freddie asked me what I was doing at the Empire Room, I told him I was going to photograph Carroll Shanks, the CEO of Prudential Insurance Company of America, *not just* CEO of the Chicago home office, but CEO of the whole works.

Freddie got to Carol Channing before her performance, so that, after her first song, she announced to the delighted audience, "We are honored to have Carroll Shanks with us tonight. He is the CEO of the Prudential Insurance Company. Not just for the regional home office, but for the whole shebang!" She then sang *"Diamonds Are a Girl's Best Friend"* and threw imitation diamond bracelets around the room as she does when she sings that song, with many landing on the Shanks party's table. I didn't ask Freddie to do that but it sure didn't hurt my relationship with Prudential.

One time the Palmer House was having a luncheon to honor the "Mother of the Year" and I was to photograph her. A man relatively new to this country by the name of Victor Borge was to present her with a bouquet of roses. I had never heard of him. When it came time to present the roses Borge kept pricking his fingers on the thorns and wincing and apologizing. The audience—including me—couldn't stop laughing. He stole the show.

Another time, after Carl Sandburg had written *Abraham Lincoln: The War Years*, I was to photograph him in Marshall Field's book department. While we were waiting and making small talk, he asked me if I knew who Edward Steichen was. Of course I knew who that world-famous photographer was. But I didn't know at the time he was Sandburg's brother-in-law. He asked me if I had bought Steichen's new book, *The Family of Man*. I said no. "I didn't think so," Sandburg replied, chuckling. "It's too damn expensive."

When I was photographing the first Mayor Daley in his office with a group of dancers from Paris, I dropped a flash bulb on the carpet. One of the dancers picked it up for me, and I said, "Merci beaucoup." The dancers, all excited, surrounded me and, thinking I knew their language, began throwing questions at me in French about Chicago. It was embarrassing when I had to confess to their interpreter that that phrase was about all I knew of the French language.

I loved the variety of shooting something different every day. But I never dreamed I would soon be photographing wild and domestic animals, celebrities like Dean Martin and Jerry Lewis, Danny Thomas, Peggy Lee, Mel Tormé, Nina Foch, Everett Edward Horton, Arthur Treacher, the entire Chicago White Sox baseball team and dozens more, each drinking milk.

GK in the leopard cage of John Cuneo, Jr.'s Animal Act, 1949 (Photo by John Cuneo, Jr.)

CHAPTER FIVE

Hawthorn Mellody

On one of my assignments, I met a new public relations man in town by the name of Carl Snyder. He had just landed a job as personal P.R. man for John F. Cuneo, Sr., who, at the time, was probably one of the five wealthiest men in Chicago.

Cuneo, Sr. was not only a friend of William Randolph Hearst (he printed all of Hearst's magazines at his huge Cuneo Press) but he had also made a fortune in real estate. He was also a director of the biggest bank in Chicago at the time, the Continental Illinois National Bank and Trust Company.

Even so, Carl complained that he was having trouble getting Cuneo's publicity photos placed in the newspapers. I said, "Maybe you're using the wrong photographer?" and suggested he try Photo Ideas, the photo studio owned by my friend Vern Whaley, who was also the picture editor of the *Chicago Herald American* newspaper. He did and immediately began having better luck.

Most times when he called Photo Ideas I was the photographer they sent. Carl and I quickly became good friends. Because we worked so well together I was soon working directly for him. Vern Whaley wasn't upset because I brought in the business in the first place, and Carl still used Photo Ideas when I wasn't available.

Until I met Carl, I didn't realize who John F. Cuneo, Sr. was but I soon learned he was a real-life tycoon whose feet never touched the ground. In the morning he would step into his limousine at his Libertyville estate (about 25 miles north of Chicago) and be driven to his offices at the Cuneo Press on the near West Side.[1]

The Cuneo Libertyville villa and surrounding Hawthorn Mellody Farms dairy had been built by Samuel Insull, the utilities tycoon and close friend of Thomas Edison. Insull went broke in 1932; in 1937, Cuneo bought the entire property—villa, farms and dairy—for $752,000, and instantly this print and real estate tycoon became the third largest supplier of milk to Chicago.

He learned the dairy business quickly but by 1944, was not happy with National Tea Company, the supermarket chain that distributed his Hawthorn Mellody milk. As one of National's largest shareholders, he audited the company's books and didn't like what he saw. With about $2 million worth of stock he gained control of the board, and in 1945, engineered a takeover, cleaned house, installed a new slate of executives and new selling practices, and was able to revitalize National Tea Company. (Ten years later, he sold National for $22 million.)

He brought this same laser-like business sense to Hawthorn Mellody Farms.

I had never seen anything like the estate. The main house was a large, two-story Italian-style villa, a virtual palace. The center courtyard with its huge skylight made you feel as though you were outdoors. The bedrooms opened onto an inside balcony that ran around the entire second floor of the courtyard.

Several large rooms on the first floor included a banquet hall that seated 65,[2] a music room, and Cuneo's own private chapel, actually a small, beautiful Catholic church that was consecrated in 1941.

Down below—I can't call it a basement—was an indoor swimming pool and large wine cellar. Outside was a very large pool and patios. As you drove up the driveway from the highway, you'd often see white deer running across the lawn.

Other buildings on the grounds included a large stable and tack room where Cuneo kept his riding horses and Hackney ponies. No horse ever had it so good. You could eat off the stable floor.

---

[1] Years later, the vacant Cuneo Press was burned to the ground, on purpose, for Ron Howard's movie *Backdraft*. I felt sad when I saw the movie, remembering Cuneo's huge, elegant office with its Oriental rugs and gorgeous furniture.

[2] Mr. and Mrs. Cuneo used a Princess telephone at each end of the table to speak to each other during large dinner parties.

Another building held Cuneo's collection of antique coaches and buggies. One of his favorites was the coach Commodore Vanderbilt used to ride to his office on Wall Street. Still another building held an indoor riding arena large enough to accommodate a circus. There was also a large greenhouse where Cuneo's gardener would coax flowers into early bloom for special occasions.

Hawthorn Mellody Farms was divided into two areas. One area was Cuneo's private estate. The other area was devoted to prize farm animals where Cuneo raised hogs, chickens, turkeys and even ducks.

But by far, the most important feature of his farm were the prize Holstein cows. Though the public wasn't allowed on the private estate, Cuneo wanted to bring people out to the farm to see his beautiful cows so they'd go home and buy Hawthorn Mellody milk. Of course, his farm supplied only a fraction of the milk to the Hawthorn Mellody Dairy. Most of it came from neighboring Illinois and Wisconsin farms.

Cuneo's brilliant idea to attract people to the farm was to build a state-of-the-art milking parlor. Enclosed in glass, the parlor was a large room with a stage on one side. Ten cows would be marched onstage, and each would be connected to an automatic milking machine. After being milked, the cows were marched out and a new group of ten would come in and be connected. Visitors were also allowed to go into the barns and see the cows up close.

These days it sounds kind of corny, but at the time, shortly after WWII, there were very few free attractions for a Chicago family who wanted to spend a Sunday afternoon in the country. The milking parlor was a huge and instant success. Many adults and children on field trips came during the week but on Sundays thousands came to see the cows being milked, overflowing the parking lot. At times, police had to direct traffic out on the highway. I was at the farm almost every Sunday shooting pictures for publicity and advertising.

The attraction continued to be popular for a couple of years, but then Cuneo came up with another brilliant idea. He would build a children's petting zoo where kids could pick up and play with small animals and see some of the larger ones in cages.

This was a huge project and would require a lot of photography. I was happy even though it is a known fact that kids and animals are not the easiest subjects to photograph. But before I tell you about the zoo, I want to tell you a little about the Cuneo family because eventually I would photograph all of them in their different worlds.

If you can remember some of the old movies from the '30s and '40s about very rich families, this was like one of those films. The tycoon father, the socialite mother, and the two young-adult interesting children.

Cuneo Sr., a short, stocky man with a pleasant demeanor, was very influential in the Catholic Church. As I mentioned, he had a private chapel in the house. On Sundays he liked to ride around his estate in one of his antique carriages pulled by a beautiful pair of matched Hackney ponies. Often his guest would be a cardinal or an archbishop or someone like William Randolph Hearst or John Ringling North.

John Cuneo, Sr. and guest on a Sunday drive with his team of Hackney ponies, 1950

Mrs. Julia (Shepherd) Cuneo, was a cordial woman whose primary interest was fashion and so I shot several of her charity fashion shows. I photographed daughter Consuela's graduation from Sacred Heart Academy and the party afterward. It was right out of Hollywood, complete with flowers, dazzling china and silverware, maids, butlers, and other assorted servants. I expected to see Jimmy Stewart walk in any minute.

Left to right (l-r) (Mrs.) Julia Cuneo, Consuela Cuneo and John Cuneo, Sr., circa 1950; John Cuneo, Jr. and bear in training session, 1950

The son, John (Johnny) Cuneo, Jr., had one overriding ambition in life: to be the world's greatest animal trainer. He was in charge of getting all the animals for the zoo. We worked closely together, photographing the animals as they arrived and then taking plenty of publicity shots after the zoo was finished.

I soon learned how deeply involved Johnny was with the animals. I knew he owned horses, but one day he took me out to a section of the farm I didn't even know existed. Here were several large cages with big black bears in them!

I said, "These are for a petting zoo?" Johnny then showed me an outdoor ring and specially built bikes and scooters for the bears to ride. He explained that the bears were not for the zoo but for his performing bear act that he had been working on for quite a while. Johnny was a few years younger than I was so he must have started training animals when he was a teenager.

He had the bears do a few tricks for me and asked if I was interested in photographing them later for a brochure. Of course I was. I don't think I ever said I didn't know how to shoot something if money was involved.

And that was the start of my Animal Period, which would include a lot more than just bears. Johnny was knowledgeable about all animals. It probably didn't hurt that a close Cuneo family friend was John Ringling North, of Ringling Bros. Circus fame. It was obvious to all of us that Johnny's whole life would be involved with animals.

While the zoo was being built we also began photographing some of the smaller animals with small kids to announce the coming of the zoo. I could handle that. But Johnny had also assembled baby lions, a cheetah, an anteater, deer, a yak, buffalo, exotic birds and more. The biggest attraction was a baby elephant that the children could ride.

Being a city boy, there were times when I needed help catching and holding down the animal to be photographed. So I told Johnny Cuneo that, if he would help me do that, I would photograph him performing with his favorite dressage horses for nothing.

John Cuneo, Jr. and dressage horse, 1950

It worked out fine. But Cuneo, Sr. always reviewed the zoo bills presented to him by Carl Snyder. One day he commented on a rather large photography bill. He said, "You should get the guy Junior uses. He does it free." Snyder laughed and told him, "Same guy."

Left to right; Press party at the Tavern Club, 1951; (l-r) Guests Vern Whaley, John Cuneo, Jr., and Mary Hartline

Cuneo, Sr. held a press party to announce the opening of the zoo at the very exclusive Tavern Club in Chicago. Junior brought the baby elephant and I brought the beautiful, blonde Mary Hartline, the star of *"Super Circus,"* a very popular children's TV show. It was the first—and last—time an elephant visited the Tavern Club. He sat on his hind legs, bowed to the crowd, shook "trunk" with people and delighted everybody. But many members of the club were not amused to learn an elephant had been on the premises. Even so, the press party was a great success.

The grand opening of the Farm Zoo was a P.R. man's dream. Kids and animals. It wasn't quite my dream because kids and animals rarely do what you ask of them, but we had no major problems. The zoo was an instant success. And it was situated next to the milking parlor so people could also watch the cows being milked. Both free attractions drew such crowds, the parking lot had to be enlarged.

Besides photographing zoo animals I did several other animal projects. With the help of farm employees I learned a lot about photographing animals. One day, Cuneo, Sr. asked me if I knew how to shoot Hereford cattle. He was selling some of his prize Herefords and was putting together a catalog with pictures. "Sure," I said. (I barely knew what a Hereford was.) He told me to see Bob, the man in charge of the cattle barn, who would bring out the cattle to be photographed.

Bob led out the first one. He was also carrying a shovel. When he asked, "Where do you want me to dig the hole?" I didn't know what he was talking about. He then explained how to photograph Herefords.

First, dig a shallow hole in the ground and position the animal's hind feet in it. That makes his back look straight. Then, pile hay on the ground until it almost touches the animal's belly. This makes him look well-fed and healthy. Now he is ready to be photographed. Bob said everyone does it that way, so all cow pictures look pretty much alike. I did it that way, too, and Cuneo, Sr. was happy with the photos.

Another time he asked me to photograph some of his prize saddle horses for a sale catalog. Of course, I knew how. (I said.) The horse trainer told me to hold on to the horse while he got the can and the ginger. "What for?" I asked, again clueless. "Well," he explained, "The horse needs to have his ears and tail up when you shoot. So you get the horse in position, then rub some ginger on his behind. This makes his tail go up. Next you rattle the can with stones in it. This makes his ears go up. Then you shoot very fast while everything is in place." It worked.

Besides shooting Junior Cuneo's trained bears, I also photographed his brand new circus act. Six leopards and six white German shepherds performed simultaneously in the same cage, an unprecedented act of animal species cooperation. There was never a dull moment at Hawthorn Mellody Farms.

After a couple of years of running ads of kids and animals, Cuneo, Sr. had another great idea. He decided to run a half-page ad in the *Chicago Daily News* rotogravure section each week. Each ad would feature a celebrity drinking Hawthorn Mellody milk, and, if possible, be photographed out at the zoo with one of the animals.

The celebrities would receive no money for doing this, but the ad would give them a free plug for wherever they were appearing in town, for their latest movie, or for whatever they wanted. Try to do that today.

Carl Snyder and I were in charge of getting the celebrities. I knew many P.R. people and contacted every one. We lined up almost every celebrity in Chicago, every movie star who came through, and whoever was performing in a show. Getting talent to cooperate turned out to be a lot easier than I thought. It got to the point where people felt slighted if they *weren't* asked to do a milk ad.

Of course, my incentive was that I got to shoot all the ads. It looked like things were going to be lucrative so I bought a new car: a brand-new 1949 maroon Plymouth Special Deluxe Club Coupe. It cost $1648 plus tax, and had a spotlight.

Here is a partial list of people I lined up for the ads and how the shoot went:

Danny Thomas. As I said in the beginning, Danny not only made the 45 minute drive out to the zoo with me, where we shot a milk ad and him judging a calf competition, but on the way back downtown, for a half hour, he helped me change a flat tire on my brand new Plymouth Deluxe. Talk about embarrassment! And after all that, he bought me dinner and a show at the Chez Paree. That's a prince.

Peggy Lee. I had photographed the perennially popular singer, songwriter and actress several times when she was in Chicago. After one publicity shoot, we were trying to get a cab in front of Marshall Field's on Wabash Avenue. She was so

Peggy Lee, 1950

stunningly beautiful, she stopped traffic just by standing there! When we asked her to do a milk ad while she was appearing at the Civic Opera House, there was no problem. What an angel.

Early on, she had learned that the softer she sang ballads, the sooner the audience quieted down to hear her. It happened when she spoke, too. I'll never forget that sweet voice. I can't believe she could ever yell at anyone. To see her, to hear her, to photograph her, there was no-one like her.

Peggy Lee was just one of the stars managed by Carlos Gastel, the famous Honduran-born Hollywood agent. Gastel also handled Nat "King" Cole, Mel Tormé, and Dean Martin and Jerry Lewis. And when one of his clients came to Chicago, my friend, Dick LaPalm, would handle their local publicity. That made it easy for me.

Mel Tormé. I had met him earlier through LaPalm. He was a real ball of energy. Originally from Chicago, he had relatives and many friends living here. He was in town appearing at the famous Blue Note but was also here to be married to Candy Toxton, a beautiful movie actress. I went to several of their pre-wedding parties.

At one of them, Mel saw a beautiful switchblade knife I had bought in Italy when I was in the Merchant Marine. Mel said he really needed it for his gun collection. It was pretty late and at the time it seemed to make sense, so I gave him the knife. Another late night, I remember a bunch of us were packed into Mike Shea's Buick convertible. I asked the girl on my lap what she did. "I'm a Goldwyn Girl," she said. If my friends from Farragut High could see me now!

There was always fun when Tormé was around. His wedding was held in a private suite at the Ambassador East Hotel. Mike Shea was to shoot the wedding and I would help. It was a Jewish wedding with all the rituals but it was not a big wedding. In addition to Mel's parents and several relatives, the invited guests included Carlos Gastel, two young female members of Mel's fan club, a few show people and Nat Cole and his wife, Maria.

Now this was February, 1949, and we all heard the whispers that management was upset about having "colored people" as wedding guests in the Ambassador East. Mel didn't care. He wanted Nat and his wife there, period. What he didn't want was a lot of newspaper photographers around but they showed up anyway. Though he didn't let them in, he compromised. Each paper gave me a film holder, and I shot a picture with my Speed Graphic camera and returned the holder. The newspapers weren't happy, but they had no choice. Mike shot all the other wedding pictures for Tormé.

Later, I shot a Hawthorn Mellody milk ad with Mel in his dressing room while he was appearing at the Chicago Theatre. Since Mel was also a serious drummer, he asked me to take a picture of him onstage while he performed with a new set of drums.

I said, "They don't allow flash bulbs in the theater." He said, "Not to worry. I cleared it with the management." So I went to one of the side balconies and prepared to take the photograph. As soon as I was spotted with a flash gun, I was escorted rapidly out of the theater. I guess Mel forgot to clear it.

Dean Martin and Jerry Lewis, 1950

Martin and Lewis. Dick LaPalm lined up Dean Martin and Jerry Lewis while they were appearing at the Chicago Theatre at the height of their popularity. I shot them in their dressing room, too, with a carton of Hawthorn Mellody milk. I can see why everyone loved Dean Martin. He was a real sweet guy. Dean: "What do

Nat "King" Cole, 1950

you want me to do?" Jerry: "Here's how we should do it." Jerry wasn't obnoxious. He had good ideas, but he liked to be in control. We got some very funny shots, and everyone was happy.

Nat "King" Cole. What a sweet guy. LaPalm arranged for me to shoot Nat for a milk ad during his appearance at the Regal Theater. "What do you want me to do? No problem." He's the kind of person I like to shoot. He talked about his happy days growing up in Chicago and about his children, Natalie and Carol. Afterwards, we sent the kids a lot of Hawthorn Mellody ice cream.

Left to right; Chet Roble, for DownBeat *magazine cover, April 6, 1951; Mary Hartline and Chet Roble, 1950*

Chet Roble. Chet was one of my closest friends. I first met him at the Cairo Lounge (Sheridan and Broadway on the North Side) where he appeared playing the piano with his Chet Roble Trio. Later, he soloed at the piano bar outside the Well of the Sea restaurant at the Sherman Hotel. Chet had a great following, including me. He called us the "Barefoot Bunch," and he gave out membership cards. I still have mine. He called his style "Barefoot Jazz."

Everybody loved Chet. He was always ready to do you a favor. Naturally, he was one of the early milk ads. And because he knew everyone, he helped me line up other people for the ads, among them Studs Terkel, Mary Hartline, Johnny Desmond, Buff Cobb and Vaughn Monroe.

One day Chet was talking about *DownBeat,* the musician's magazine and said how much he'd like to be in it. I said, "We can do that." We went over to Music Corporation of America (MCA), which was Chet's agent. There, in a studio with a large grand piano, Chet played for about a half hour while I shot pictures.

I took the best ones over to *DownBeat.* I had never done anything for the magazine or knew anyone working there. But I handed the pictures to the editor and said, "Chet should be on the cover." *DownBeat* liked the pictures, interviewed him, and a couple of weeks later, Chet was on the cover, with a great story on him inside. I could never do that today.

At one point during the early '50s, Chet and Mary Hartline hosted a popular daytime TV show for kids, *"Aunt Mary and Uncle Chet."* They would sing songs and play games. We used to laugh about it off camera. Mary looked like a Petty Girl and Chet referred to himself as a saloon piano player, but the kids loved the show.

Buff Cobb. Mike Wallace (yes, of *"60 Minutes"*) and his wife, Buff Cobb, were doing a nightly radio show from the Chez Paree. I didn't know Mike but Chet did. He got Mike on the phone, and then I explained that I wanted to shoot his wife for a milk ad. No problem. We set up a date, and I photographed her in their apartment around the corner from the Ambassador East. Just about everyone who was anybody lived close to the Ambassador East. Buff Cobb was very gracious. Everyone should be so easy to shoot.

Chet soon became a permanent member of the cast of the TV show, *"Studs' Place."* Chet introduced me to Studs Terkel, the star and creator, and guess who would soon be sitting on the *"Studs' Place"* set with a quart of Hawthorn Mellody milk?

Studs Terkel. I liked Studs immediately. He was extremely smart, his show was a big success, and I was thrilled to get him posing with the milk. He always had other things going on, too. On his popular radio show, *"The Wax Museum,"* Studs would play any and all types of music—folk music, opera, jazz, or blues— and talk knowledgably about all of them. He was also an actor and frequently appeared on stage in Chicago.

Studs Terkel on the set of "Studs' Place," 1950

I often went to the set to watch *"Studs' Place"* as it was being televised live. I wonder if Studs ever noticed the full Muriel cigar boxes in his display case on the set? At the time, I was doing work for P. Lorillard, the makers of Old Gold cigarettes and Muriel cigars. Many times before the show, Chet and I would sneak boxes of Muriel cigars into the glass display case by the cash register. It certainly cemented my relations with Lorillard. You could do things like that in those days.

Nina Foch. We photographed this accomplished, poised and beautiful film and stage actress long before her Oscar nomination *("Executive Suite")* and role as patron and paramour of Gene Kelly in *"An American In Paris."* For our shoot, she was feeding a bear cub from a baby bottle and was totally cooperative, even when the bear scratched her! Today, we would probably get sued.

Nina Foch, 1950

Guy Kibbey. If you've ever seen *"Mr. Smith Goes to Washington,"* you'd recognize him as Governor Hubert "Happy" Hopper. He was a talented character actor who appeared in 114 movies during a 60-year show-business career that began at age 13, when he performed on a Mississippi river boat. When I photographed him, he was in his 70s and still going strong. He had no trouble holding on to the horns of the billy goat we brought out to shoot him with.

Jeffrey Lynn. He had just starred in the Oscar-winning *"A Letter to Three Wives"* with Jeanne Crain, Kirk Douglas and Paul Douglas and we were really happy to get him. I shot him with a tiny Central American squirrel monkey. The picture was fine, but Lynn, who was a really sharp dresser, would have looked better wearing a pith helmet and safari shirt instead of a jacket, dress shirt and plaid bow-tie. I should have brought them with me.

John Loder, 1950

John Loder. I was expecting the handsome English actor who was Hedy Lamarr's ex-husband, a former German prisoner of WWI and who appeared in Paramount's first talking motion picture, to be suave and debonair. Most of the time, he probably was but I think we got him too early in the morning. He looked a bit rumpled but was very polite and did whatever I asked. I photographed him with a duck and the picture was fine.

Arthur Treacher, 1951

Arthur Treacher. British-born, Treacher was considered the "perfect butler" by Hollywood, playing Jeeves in two movies based on that P.G. Wodehouse character. (Later, he lent his name to a 500-store fast food chain known as Arthur Treacher's Fish and Chips.) I was always a great fan of his and especially loved the sour puss he put on to express disdain. In fact, that sparked my idea to shoot him with a skunk. He couldn't have been more cooperative. When I convinced him the skunk was deodorized he agreed to hold it up by the tail (not an authorized move by today's PETA standards) and to give me that wonderful disdainful look. It's one of my favorite pictures.

Edward Everett Horton, 1950

Edward Everett Horton. He was appearing in a play downtown but we convinced him to come out to the farm zoo. That way I got to talk with him on the drive out and back. Over a 60-year career, he made 120 movies, silent films at the beginning and then his first "talkie," *"The Front Page,"* a Chicago-based movie written by Ben Hecht and Charlie MacArthur. Later, he appeared in six of the Fred Astaire and Ginger Rogers movies. (Horton keeps showing up on Turner Classic Movies in case you're a fan.)

I photographed him flirting with a small guinea pig and vice versa. As we drove back downtown on Lake Shore Drive, Horton pointed out a building where a friend of his lived, Mrs. Josephine Logan, who founded an organization called "Sanity in Art." I told him my father was also a friend of hers and was a member of her organization. We were both thrilled. It's a small world.

Jimmy Dorsey. One of the top big band leaders in the country, Jimmy was appearing with his Jimmy Dorsey Orchestra at the Marine dining room of the Edgewater Beach Hotel on Chicago's North Side. That beautiful one-of-a-kind hotel was a jewel, with its own private beach on Lake Michigan and outdoor dining. During the summer, people with boats would anchor right off the hotel and listen to the music from the big bands.

I was truly excited to meet Jimmy: a one-time child prodigy who was also a virtuoso on the trumpet, alto sax and clarinet and who had played with such jazz greats as Bix Beiderbecke, "Red" Nichols, Pee Wee Russell, Sidney Bechet, Bobby Hackett, Bunny Berigan and Bud Freeman, to name a few. He had also composed dozens of songs, including pop hits *"I'm Glad There Was You"* (with Paul Madeira) and *"So Rare."*

We arranged to meet in the bar before his first set. We had a drink and I explained what I wanted to do in the photo. No problem. He was another winner. While I was shooting we talked about music and I told him how much I liked Dixieland, not knowing that he often took a small group out of his orchestra and played heated Dixieland.

He said, "Stay for the second show. I have to play all the slow stuff for the first show." And during the second show, he played wonderful, hot Dixieland. What a guy.

I know I keep talking about how nice everyone was to me, but it's true. The only person who ever gave me trouble was **Mae West,** but it wasn't really trouble. She agreed to endorse the milk but wouldn't allow her picture to be taken. She insisted on furnishing her own photo, which we used. I could see why. She was getting on in years and had put on a few pounds. The picture she gave us was retouched to give her a much slimmer waist. That was OK. She was still a star.

Vaughn Monroe. I shot the famous baritone *("Racing With the Moon")* and band leader (who had a string of 75 chart hits in 14 years) a few months later, also at the Edgewater Beach Hotel. Again, there was no problem. "Where and when do you want me?" he asked. We made a date for the next afternoon. I set up my camera and quart of milk. He showed up on time. What more could I ask?

Johnny Desmond. While in the army he had been a singer with the Glenn Miller Orchestra and was known as the G.I.'s Sinatra. When I met Johnny (through Chet Roble), he was a singer on *"Don McNeill's Breakfast Club,"* a very popular morning radio show in Chicago. He was happy to do the milk ad. He, too, lived around the corner from the Ambassador East Hotel. He had two young daughters and suggested we put them in the photo with him. This made a lot of sense. I shot the three of them in his apartment, and Hawthorn Mellody milk never looked better.

Johnny Desmond and daughters, circa 1952

I shot Johnny on other occasions and we became friends. A few years later, he moved to New York and really hit it big. At one time he was starring in a Broadway play, *"Say, Darling."* He was also the lead singer, along with Dorothy Collins, on

"Lucky Strike Hit Parade" rehearsal;
(l-r) Norman Jewison (back to camera),
Alan Jay Lerner, Dorothy Collins, Johnny
Desmond and Frederick Loewe, 1958

the *"Lucky Strike Hit Parade"* television show, directed by Norman Jewison.[3] Plus he had a Saturday morning radio show with Tony Matola and other musicians. I went to New York to do a feature story on him.

At his house in Manhasset, Long Island, I shot Johnny, his family and the Jaguar XK 120 that he drove his girls to school in. In New York on the set of the *"Hit Parade,"* I met and photographed the guests that week: lyricist Alan Jay Lerner and composer Frederick Loewe, creators of the Broadway hits *"My Fair Lady,"* *"Camelot," "Brigadoon," "Gigi"* and *"Paint Your Wagon."*

I got really good pictures of the incredibly talented Peter Gennaro, choreographer for the show, who was coaching Johnny on dance steps for that week's performance.

Then I met the cast of *"Say, Darling"* that included Vivian Blaine, David Wayne, Bobby Morse (TV's *Mad Men)* and Jerome Cowan. I don't know how Johnny kept track of everything he was doing, but he did. I was happy to see him doing so well, but I was exhausted following him around.

---

3 Later, Jewison's Hollywood hits would number 50 films, including *"The Russians Are Coming, The Russians Are Coming," "In The Heat of the Night," "Fiddler on the Roof," "Jesus Christ, Superstar"* and *"A Soldier's Story."*

(l-r) Peter Gennaro and Johnny Desmond, 1958

Dick Contino, 1950

Dick Contino. "The world's greatest accordionist" came out to the farm with his accordion, his father and his P.R. man. They were more interested in Cuneo's estate than in the milk. I had Dick sit on the rail of a horse corral with his accordion and was ready to shoot when Johnny Cuneo came by riding one of his performing horses.

Johnny asked Dick if he knew how to play that thing—the accordion. Dick said, "I think so." I forget the song that Johnny asked him to play, but Johnny's horse did a little dance to the music. After we introduced everyone, Johnny thanked Dick for the music and rode off. I think that was probably the only time Dick Contino played for a horse.

Flame. We even used four-legged celebrities for milk ads. Flame was the most beautiful German Shepherd I'd ever seen. He was a famous movie dog from Hollywood, in town to promote his latest movie, *"Pal's Gallant Journey."* How could we use him? Carl had a great idea. Cuneo, Sr. had a Grand Champion Holstein bull that he wanted to appear in one of the ads. "Let's work Flame in with the champion bull," Carl suggested. "The bull has a trophy. Let's have the movie-star dog present the trophy to the champion bull."

I picked up Flame and his trainer in front of the Merchandise Mart where they had just appeared on a TV show. A crowd surrounded the limping and moaning Flame, who was putting on a show for the people at the Mart. When the trainer saw me he snapped his fingers. Flame immediately stood up, took a bow and jumped in the back seat of my car. I drove out to the farm with his cold nose pressing on the back of my neck the whole way. I didn't mind. Flame was such a great dog.

At the farm they rigged up a handle around the trophy so that Flame could hold it in his mouth. I wasn't worried about Flame, but a Holstein bull is not a petting animal. It is big and powerful and not a movie actor. I had seen that bull bend bars in his stall when he wasn't happy. I was nervous.

Champion Holstein bull and Flame, the movie star dog, 1951

We set up a place to shoot, put Flame in place, and brought out the bull. I was ready. Flame was ready, the trophy in his mouth. The farm hands walked the bull up to Flame, leading him by the ring in his nose. I don't know what the bull was thinking but he just stared at Flame while I shot very fast. I was happy when that shoot was over.

Sid Luckman. The Chicago Bears' famous quarterback was retired and owned an auto dealership on Chicago's West Side. He figured it wouldn't hurt to give his dealership a plug in a milk ad. Sid asked only that I put a little statue of a bear next to the milk carton. Which we did.

Kay Westfall. Some of you may remember Kay as the original *"Lucille in her merry Oldsmobile"* in the early Oldsmobile TV commercials. She also hosted a very popular Chicago daytime TV show with Bob Murphy called *"The Bob & Kay Show"* doing interviews and local chatter. When I told Kay about Cuneo and the zoo, she suggested, "Why not have Johnny Cuneo bring one of the animals on the show and we'll 'interview' him?" That sounded great.

Kay Westfall, 1951

I told Johnny about it and said maybe he should bring an animal that would drink milk during the interview. We'd really *milk* the interview. Johnny agreed and we set up a date with Kay. I was to meet him at the ABC-TV studio, located on the top floor of the Civic Opera House. In fact, it was the former penthouse apartment of Samuel Insull, the man who built the Opera House.

Johnny showed up on time. I was waiting for him and almost fell through the floor when he stepped off the freight elevator with a 200-pound bear. Johnny swore the bear was safe. Bob and Kay did a very nervous interview interviewing Johnny, while the bear sat in a chair alongside them drinking "milk" out of a Hawthorn Mellody carton. Johnny had brought the milk carton for the bear to drink from but didn't tell Kay and Bob there was honey, not milk, inside. But it looked really good in the pictures!

Kay was a beautiful woman with a perfect figure. I wanted her to appear in a milk ad, but Carl said, "She looks so good, let's use her instead with Vita Slim," which was Hawthorn Mellody's skim milk. That was fine with me. I took her out to the estate and shot her on the diving board of the Cuneo's swimming pool. We all knew it would take more than Vita Slim to have a body like hers.

Herb Shriner. Herb was a popular humorist with *"Herb Shriner Time,"* a CBS Radio weekday program in 1948 and '49 and a national TV show, *"Herb Shriner Show"* in 1956. As I said before, no one was safe from the milk ad group. I don't think Shriner had ever heard of Hawthorn Mellody milk, but while he was appearing at the Chez Paree, he agreed to do the ad. He turned out to be a very nice man, even when I referred to him as a comedian. He gently corrected me. "I am not a comedian. I am a humorist."

I spent some time with him and his lovely wife Eileen "Pixie" Shriner before the shoot. We had a couple of drinks and Herb told me he was thinking of going into the movie business. I really liked the Shriners. The shoot went well, and I hoped to see them again. Unfortunately, in 1970, when Herb was at his peak, they were both killed in an auto accident in Florida. They were riding in one of Shriner's antique cars, a Studebaker Avanti, when the brakes failed. They left three children: a daughter Indy and twin sons Wil Shriner and Kin Shriner.

Herb Shriner, 1950

The White Sox. I shot many more celebrities for the ads, but most of those shoots went so smoothly I hardly remember doing them. I must remind you that no one got paid to do the ads—with one exception. The Chicago White Sox baseball team. I forgot whether it was Carl or Cuneo's ad agency that lined up the team who agreed to do the ads for $100 for each player.

So one day Carl and I went out to Comiskey Park and before, after, and during the game I shot most of the team individually. They were either drinking, pouring, or just holding a glass of milk. As soon as I would shoot one player, Carl would have them sign a release saying none of them endorsed any other milk. It was a very busy and productive afternoon.

Nellie Fox,
Chicago White Sox star
second baseman and Baseball
Hall of Famer, 1950

The ball players were a lot of fun. They made jokes about the milk. Most of them chewed tobacco and were constantly spitting. I had to remind them not to drink the milk with tobacco in their mouths.

We had a good time even though I was hit in the ankle by a foul ball while I was sitting on a bench against the wall. It wasn't serious, and I was glad it was me and not the camera that got it. We found out later a few of the players had already endorsed the Bowman Dairy. Well, what do you expect for $100?

American Airline stewardesses. This was the time when the women who worked on the airlines were called stewardesses. They had to be young, single, and good-looking.

The P.R. woman at American Airlines suggested we use some of the stewardesses in the milk ads. It was a great idea. We couldn't find a Danny Thomas or a Martin and Lewis every week, and what's wrong with young, beautiful girls in sharp uniforms drinking milk? We used several of them in the ads and they really looked good in their uniforms. It was the era of long skirts. Today, some of the pictures look dated, but at the time we were all happy with the results.

I'm not sure why I got along so well with all these celebrities, but I think part of it was that I was never in awe of them and never asked for an autograph. I did admire them. We always had interesting conversations. Part of it, too, was that they were much more at ease with a photographer than a reporter with a pad and pencil or tape recorder. Photographers don't take notes. And finally, I think they realized that I really liked them. We always had fun. I don't think any of them had ever done a milk ad before. In fact, I also suspect many of them didn't even drink milk and that was part of the fun.

I would do other projects later on for the Cuneos, but the milk ads were one of my favorite projects of all time. You could never do them today the way we did them then.

FINANCE

All the News of the Hire of the Dollar

FINANCE Photo by George Kufrin

John D. Allen, Chairman of the Board, Brink's, Inc. (SEE PAGE 29)

MID-YEAR COMPILATION OF CORRESPONDENT BANK BALANCES

(SEE PAGE 27)

AUGUST 15, 1954   50 Cents Per Copy

Finance *cover of Brink's chairman, John. D. Allen, 1954*

CHAPTER SIX

Finance Magazine

In May of 1941, Reuben A. Lewis, Jr., an energetic, ambitious 46-year old native son of Birmingham, Alabama, fulfilled a lifelong dream. The one-time bureau chief of the *Journal of Commerce* in New York, former vp of the Continental Illinois National Bank in Chicago and executive vp of Metropolitan Trust bought *The Chicago Banker,* a venerable Chicago business weekly which had been publishing continuously since 1898. Lewis' plan? Bring in top national finance writers like Merryle Rukeyser as associate editor and Theodore Goldsmith as Washington correspondent, redesign and rename the magazine *Finance* and publish it weekly from Chicago.

The first issue rolled off the presses on September 25, 1941, two months before Pearl Harbor. By the third issue, Lewis had decided to publish bi-weekly.

Throughout the trying and terrible years of the war, Lewis proved to be a colorful and persistent editor and publisher, concentrating on three things: businessmen with unusual and newsworthy American success stories, the government's use of private money, and publishing specialized financial information not found in other publications. When he died suddenly at 52 of cancer, his widow, southern-born Mohan Catherine Richardson Lewis, a devout Civil War buff who had been associate editor of *Finance,* took over as publisher, or as she put it, "lady" publisher.

By then, *Finance,* though small, had become a very successful operation. Most important, Mohan carried on the Lewis tradition after his death, running feature stories on the top U.S. financial institutions and digging "like a terrier for the glamour and color" Lewis regarded as a vital part of the national financial scene. She also featured unusual and newsworthy American success stories about financial giants of the time and hired free-lance writers and photographers from New York to do them.

Shortly before he died in 1948, Lewis had hired Sam Burton Lyons to write the monthly cover story for *Finance.* Sam had a great resumé. He had worked as a correspondent and contributing editor for *Time* magazine before WWII and as a combat correspondent for *Stars and Stripes* during that war. He was later radio news editor for the Voice of America.

Born and raised in Manassas, Virginia, Sam had a southern accent, not deep South but very pleasant to listen to. Sam and his wife, Carol, had moved from New York to Geneva, Illinois, a Chicago suburb. It was a snap for Sam to do one feature each month, but after Lewis' death, he was asked to become editor and also to work for a female publisher who had very little publishing experience. Soon he was doing nearly all of the editorial work on *Finance.* He and the "lady publisher" made an intriguing combination.

Mohan treated Sam well. Perks of his job included memberships in the Union League Club, the Geneva Country Club and the Electric Club, which was a very exclusive restaurant in the Civic Opera House, the same building where Photo Ideas was based.

In 1949, I ran into Sam a couple of times at various financial meetings where I was shooting for Vern Whaley or Don Alford at INP. Sam was still using New York photographers for the big jobs at *Finance* and local photographers for the smaller ones.

One day, while we were waiting for a meeting to start, I mentioned to Sam that I didn't only shoot publicity and news pictures with my Speed Graphic. I also had a Rolleiflex and was very good at shooting magazine photos, which, of course, is a different style. I gave him my card and a couple of weeks later he called me to do a small job. He liked the results.

When I first saw *Finance,* I was impressed by its appearance: it looked like a slick *Time* magazine but was printed on better paper. Its mission, stated under the masthead, was "All the News of the Hire of the Dollar."

A few more local assignments followed that Sam was happy with. Best of all, Mohan also liked the results and she signed the checks. Several months later I was surprised to see my name on the masthead as staff photographer. I didn't have a contract, I don't remember anyone asking me if I wanted to be on the masthead, but I was certainly happy to be there.

Mohan's real name was Catherine, though she never used it. Mohan was an old family name. If someone called her "Miss Kitty" you knew it was some childhood friend or relative. She wasn't your run-of-the-mill publisher. She not only decided what would go into the magazine but she also chose the photos, did the picture layout and paste-up.

When I met her, I think she was in her early 40s. She talked softly, usually with a sarcastic tone. She hardly ever laughed, but smiled or chuckled if she liked something. She knew every major banker in the country by his first name or nickname. She could be moody. She was from the South but I'm not sure where. I wouldn't exactly call her a racist, but she did wish the South had won the Civil War. Once, to a costume party, she wore a rebel officer's uniform, sword and all.

Mohan was also deeply involved with Mary Thompson Hospital, operated entirely by female doctors. Mohan was on its board, became its president for several years and was very active in promoting and fundraising for the hospital. I met and photographed most of the doctors and was impressed with how dedicated they were, and also how much fun they were. One year, Mohan became critically ill (I don't know why), but there were women doctors around her bed 24 hours a day. I think in another hospital she may not have survived. (Mary Thompson Hospital closed its doors in 1988.)

I think Mohan and I got along well because our backgrounds were so different. I was a 23-year old former merchant seaman from the west side of Chicago. She was a Southerner, and an owner and publisher of a successful slick magazine on finance. Still, though we got along well, it was a year before I decided I liked her.

Mohan Lewis, publisher of Finance *magazine, in costume for a party, circa 1955*

Sam B. Lyons,
then editor of Finance
magazine, 1958

She was much nicer than she let on. For one thing, I never worked for anyone without having to give him or her a bill.

The system at *Finance* was for me to bring in the prints and Mohan would immediately write out a check. She decided how much. That could have been bad but her check was always more than I would have billed her for. When a picture was especially good, it would show up in the check. What a system.

Finance opened up a whole new world to me. I met different kinds of people and experienced situations and ideas I hadn't known before.

For example, working for *Finance* meant Sam and I always went first-class. We traveled all over the country, staying in the best hotels and eating in the finest restaurants. I'll never forget the first time I sent my laundry out at the Waldorf Astoria—and my socks came back *ironed*. That was a first for me.

Yes, Sam and Mohan were a great pair to work for.

Sam Lyons I had liked immediately, as did everybody who knew him. Plus he was a joy to work *with*. He knew his job and assumed I knew mine. About the only guidance he ever gave me were the names of the people to shoot. He knew everyone in the news business from his days in New York and Washington.

One day, after many years of hard drinking, he passed out and came to in a hospital. The doctors convinced him that if he kept it up he would die. He said, "I don't want to die," and never took another drink. Some years later he left *Finance* magazine, and after a short stint with an investment house he became a vice-president of the New York Stock Exchange, working in Washington, D.C., his hometown. His was a huge success story.

For years, Sam, who had become our son Ben's devoted godfather, his wife Carol and daughter Lael, and Joan, Ben, Eve and I spent Christmas together in the Florida Keys. Sam taught us to fish, his lifelong passion that became ours. He and I remained close friends until he died in 1999. I cherish his Bull & Bear tie from the N.Y. Stock Exchange that he gave me—even though I only wear bow ties.

I've lost track of the number of stories I shot for *Finance,* but the more interesting ones always involved Sam.

One of the last stories we did together involved an oil well. Sam called me one day and told me to meet him Friday morning at Midway Airport. "We're going to Texas!"

At the airport Sam introduced me to Edde K. Hays and Robert A. Podesta. Edde was the pilot and also a partner in the Dean Witter organization. We would be flying in his plane, a twin-engine Lockheed Lodestar, similar to the plane Amelia Earhart flew on her failed trip around the world. Edde could have passed for Ross Perot's brother. Same build, same voice, and the same ball of energy.

Bob Podesta was the tall, handsome-like-a-movie-star managing partner of the investment banking firm of Cruttendon and Podesta, who later founded the Chicago Corporation, Podesta & Co., and served four years as head of the Economic Development Administration under President Richard Nixon.

Oil Well, Texas National Petroleum Co., Midland, Texas, 1959

Both men's firms had money invested in the oil company that was bringing in the well. I immediately liked them both and they liked me. In fact, I would eventually photograph many of Bob Podesta's business and political activities, including his unsuccessful run for Congress in 1968.

I was even more impressed with Podesta when I learned he had begun his financial career as a runner on LaSalle Street, a job he got right out of high school during the Depression and that it took him 14 years of Northwestern University night school to finally receive his degree in business administration. We were friends until he died in 1999.

Sam would write the oil well cover story for *Finance* and I would take the pictures. We were one happy group flying to a party in Midland, Texas, to bring in an oil well.

Waiting for the well to come in. Texas National Petroleum Co., Midland, Texas, 1959

(l-r) Edde Hayes, B. Gordon, Robert Podesta, J. Johnston and S. Boyle watch oil come in at 10 barrels an hour

Edde was probably in his fifties, but he was like a little kid when he flew that plane. He actually bounced in his seat and talked to the plane as we took off. We arrived in Midland without incident and checked into the local hotel. We were going to a party that night at the Midland Country Club to celebrate bringing in the oil well. I would have thought you'd have the party *after* you bring in the well, but what did I know?

And it was quite a party, full of authentic Texas oil millionaires. The millionaire in charge of the festivities wore a white tuxedo jacket and a fancy shirt with a button-down collar. The buttons were diamonds. Sam asked him who were the more important people at the party that I should photograph? His answer was, "Boy, there ain't no clerks here."

The next morning we went out to the oil well site. I really enjoyed seeing an oil well dug and learning how important the mud is. But this was not like Hollywood movies where oil gushes out all over everybody when the well comes in. Here, after a little more drilling, someone merely turned some valves, and there was oil. I took the pictures, and then they capped the well.

While flying back to Chicago I sat in the co-pilot's seat. Edde told me he was going to buy a smaller plane. This one had a separate cabin for the pilot and he felt more like an employee than part of the group.

After that, I ran into Edde at different financial meetings. At one of them he told me he had just bought a new airplane, a twin Beach Bonanza. A *very nice* airplane." And one day, he called me and said he was flying to New York for two days in the new airplane and would I like to come along for the ride? Sounded good to me. I can always find something to do in New York.

One time I was in Hollywood, Florida, at the annual investment Bankers meeting for *Finance*. Edde had flown himself down from Chicago. The meeting was dull. "Let's take a day off and fly to Nassau and sample the night life," he suggested. So off we went: Edde, my friend Ed Darby, financial editor of the *Chicago Sun-Times*—and former White House correspondent for *Time* during the Truman and Eisenhower administrations—and I. After a great time we flew back to Hollywood the next morning, energized. No one semed to miss us.

The Investment Bankers Association convention always took place at the Hollywood Beach Hotel in Florida, an absolutely first-class hotel. Its food, service, Olympic-sized pool, and beach were the finest. A buffet lunch served daily by the pool featured lobster, shrimp, whole fish, prime beef and more, putting to shame other buffets I've known that serve pretty vegetables but little real food.

The top investment people in the country and the heads of all the major stock exchanges attended the small, exclusive IBA convention. So did the top financial writers from the nation's most influential newspapers and magazines who used the opportunity to interview the investment people non-stop.

The convention always happened in November when the weather in Florida was good. One of the best parts was getting there. We flew Delta Airlines which had a flight to Miami from Chicago they called the Champagne Flight. After the reservation was made, Delta would call your office to ask if you wanted chicken or steak for lunch. If you said steak they asked how you wanted it done. I always asked for a rare steak and it always arrived well-done. But I could live with that. Delta served all the champagne and any other drinks you wanted. More than one person was poured off the plane.

American Airlines had a similar dinner flight from New York to Chicago called the Captain's Flagship. It would leave from Gate 1 at La Guardia and pull up to Gate 1 at Chicago's Midway. Along the way, you were given little slippers for your feet. The stewardesses, wearing dresses with corsages, went down the aisle with pitchers of martinis. After a great meal, they gave you a souvenir. I still have my money clip with the American Airlines logo. Of course, all the seats were made for humans and not sardines. Is it any wonder I hate to fly now?

At the IBA convention, there was plenty of free time to play. And we did. One evening after dinner, Sam and I were sitting at the hotel bar discussing what to do that evening. There were no scheduled functions. I was reading the *Miami Herald* when I saw an ad for Lorelei the Mermaid, who was appearing at a Miami Beach club. I told Sam about it. "Who the hell is Lorelei the Mermaid?" he asked.

I told Sam *Finance* wasn't the only magazine I worked for. One of the others was *Modern Man*. Among other stories, they did features on exotic dancers. A few months earlier, I had shot a feature on Lorelei the Mermaid. In her act she emerged from a giant clamshell wrapped in a fish net. The shell was wired with flash bulbs that went off when she opened the shell. Then she would do a dance while removing the net and everything else she had on and ended her act by crawling back into the shell. It was something to see.

Since I knew her I thought it would be a nice gesture to drop in at the club and say hello. Just then, Ed Darby and Jim Day, who was the president of the Midwest Stock Exchange, came by. We had a few more drinks and told them of our plans to see Lorelei.

After still more drinks they also thought visiting Lorelei was a good idea and decided to come along. I don't remember Jim Day drinking much. Thank God, he was driving. By the time we got there, I had fallen asleep in the car and didn't feel like getting out. The other three went in and saw Lorelei. After her act they brought her out to the car to say hello to me. I was glad to see her.

The other convention we went to every year was the ABA, the American Bankers Association. It was huge, attended by thousands of bankers from all over the country and for that reason wasn't as much fun as the IBA. The appeal was that each year it was held in a different city, such as Los Angeles, San Francisco or New York.

When someone like David Rockefeller, then president of the Chase Manhattan Bank, threw a little cocktail party for 3,000 people it just didn't compare with the IBA. Plus there were too many meetings and parties to go to at the ABA.

Mohan, however, always attended the ABA convention. In 1962, it was held in Atlantic City when that city was still in its prime and a fun place to visit. She and I were to attend a luncheon at a hotel on the boardwalk. There were over-size basket chairs on the boardwalk that looked like big baby buggies and they were pushed primarily by old men. Mohan insisted we take one of those chairs to the luncheon. I felt like a real jerk being pushed by a guy who looked like he was at least 90.

But that was also the year the Mosler Safe Company stole the show. Mosler was the safe manufacturer who built the vaults for the United States gold reserves at Fort Knox, Kentucky and also the vaults used to display and safeguard the original United States Constitution and the Declaration of Independence.

Members of the Mosler family always went to the ABA conventions. Who else could you sell those huge safes to but bankers? And this year, the Moslers had engaged Sam Snead, the champion golfer (three PGA, three Masters, and one British Open wins) who was in his prime, to set up an area on one of the piers that jut out into the ocean. From there Snead could hit golf balls across the water to the beach.

The platform where Snead stood was covered with artificial grass. A banker could go up on the platform, hit a ball and Snead would tell him how to correct his swing. In short, you got a brief, free lesson from Sam Snead. What a sight! Hundreds of bankers lined up like little kids waiting for a pony ride. The downside was that many of the meetings scheduled that day were poorly attended. You can always go to a meeting, but you can't always get a free lesson from Sam Snead.

In 1955, the ABA convention was held in San Francisco. Sam wanted to look up an old friend who lived there. I said I wanted to look up a girl I knew from Chicago who had moved there. Talk about a small world. His friend was dating my friend! The four of us got together and had a great time.

We even found time to go to the U.S. Open Golf tournament. That year a municipal golf-course operator from Iowa, Jack Fleck, tied Ben Hogan on the last hole of the final round, forcing a playoff. Jack who? Unfortunately, the next day Hogan double-bogeyed the last hole, and the unknown Fleck won the tournament by three strokes, 69-72. But it was really something to see Ben Hogan and all the other great players of that era.

Reno Odlin, chairman of the Puget Sound National Bank, was a close friend of Mohan's. He aspired to be president of the American Bankers Association—lots of prestige and a one-year term. *Finance* did some cover stories on him, which helped him get elected to the post. Reno was a sharp guy and a lot of fun. He was short and stocky and had a great speaking voice. To Mohan he looked like a cherub. I loved to hear him speak. One of his favorite phrases when talking politics was "When the Emperor Caligula appointed his horse to the Roman senate, he at least appointed the whole horse."

Mohan didn't go with Sam and me on a story unless it was special or it was the annual ABA convention. When we went to Puget Sound to do a major piece on Reno, she came along. Reno really knew how to treat you well. He had a beautiful home overlooking Puget Sound, which he had nicknamed "Teetering," short for "Teetering on the Brink." In the distance you could see a federal prison that he called the "Bankers' Club."

Sam did an in-depth story on Reno and his bank and Reno was very happy with the pictures I made of him. (So was I.) At the time, Dwight Eisenhower was President and his brother, Edgar, was a director of Reno's bank. We tried to get a scoop and find out what the President's golf handicap was. But it seemed that was highly classified information. Edgar wouldn't budge on revealing it.

Reno Odlin,
chairman, Puget
Sound National Bank,
Tacoma, WA, 1954

When I returned to Chicago, I found a slip under my door from the Railway Express Agency that said they had a package for me to pick up. The only other word on the slip was "fish." I thought it was awfully nice of Reno to send me a couple of pounds of that great smoked salmon we had at his house.

I went down that night to pick up the package. When I gave the man my REA slip he got out his hand truck and walked over to a big walk-in cooler. He came out with what looked like a small coffin. In it was a huge fresh salmon packed in ice. He helped me put it in my small Hillman station wagon. I sat there awhile and wondered what the hell I was going to do with this big fish.

The fish stayed in the car that night. The next morning I took it over to Burhop's, a local wholesale and retail seafood company on State Street where I asked for advice. The manager thought it was a beautiful fish and offered to prepare it for baking. He could even have it baked since it wouldn't fit into a regular oven. And I could pick it up in two days completely prepared and baked.

This called for a party. I was living with Bob Kotalik, a *Sun-Times* photographer, in an apartment too small for a party but I had a girlfriend down the street with a larger apartment. I told her, "Call all your friends and I'll call mine. We'll have a fish party at your place." I also told Mike Shea, who told too many others. The party was a huge success even though more people came than we expected.

It reminded me of the Marx Brothers movie *"A Night at the Opera"* where many people are mashed into a small ship's cabin. When the maid opens the door, all the people fall out. I knew about half of those who came to the party. Hugh Hefner even made a brief appearance with his entourage.

I can tell you—that fish did not die in vain. People did everything but lick the platter. Thank you, Reno Odlin.

Another of those American success cover stories I did for *Finance* was on R. Crosby Kemper, Sr., who took the City National Bank in Kansas City, Missouri from a three-man operation with $600,000 in deposits in 1919 to a 700-employee institution with $300 million in deposits when he stepped down as chairman of the board in September, 1967. When *Finance* did the story in 1961, City National was the largest bank in Kansas City, and Kemper probably the richest man in town. I remember him talking about Harry Truman, saying that before Truman became president he hung out with local Kansas City ward politicians and Kemper didn't have much to do with him. But now that Truman was a former president, Kemper thought "We probably should have him over for dinner one night."

At the time, Kemper's son, R. Crosby Kemper, Jr., was running for the U.S. Senate. Also, the New York Yankees were in town to play the Kansas City A's. Kemper, Sr. asked if I would take a picture of Kemper, Jr. with Roger Maris and Mickey Mantle for his son's Senate campaign. Of course I would. So Kemper made a phone call and set it up.

Everyone I talked with said Mickey Mantle was a prince, but warned me Roger Maris would be difficult. It was the year Maris was about to break Babe Ruth's home run record and he was very unpopular. We got to the ballpark before the game with Kansas City. Mickey Mantle never showed up for the photo. But Maris was waiting.

"What do you want me to do?" he asked. We set up a couple of pictures with Kemper, Jr. and Roger Maris couldn't have been more cooperative. (So much for gossip.) I liked him very much. If I had thought to bring a dozen baseballs along, I'm sure he would have signed them. But, as I said before, I never was much of a baseball fan.

Another time, Kemper, Sr. was host to a large conference of bankers in Kansas City. The highlight of the conference was a color-animated film presentation by Dr. Wernher von Braun, the German-American rocket scientist/ aerospace engineer/ space architect who was key in the development of rocket technology in Nazi Germany but who worked for America after the war.[1] Von Braun predicted all the exploration man was going to do in space. It was a fascinating presentation but I think many people in the audience—including me—were skeptical. The material was really far out, spacewise and otherwise. Today, most of what von Braun talked about that day has already happened.

Another story I got a kick out of was going to Memphis, Tennessee, to do a piece on John Brown, chairman of Union Planters National Bank, established in 1869. His was a good story but the best part was when Brown took us to a floor in the bank that didn't look at all like a bank. It seems the bank made many loans to cotton growers. But in order to get a loan, the growers had to bring in large samples of their cotton crops, which were then left at the bank. On this un-bank-like floor the bank's own baling machine was baling the cotton samples. I don't know what a bale of cotton sells for, but it must have been profitable. I saw quite a few bales.

One of the first stories I shot for *Finance* was on Brinks, the armored car company. And one of my favorite *Finance* covers is of John D. Allen, Sr., Brinks' board chairman, standing in the doorway of a huge vault with bags of money behind him. Allen was one of those unusual and noteworthy American success stories that *Finance* loved to uncover.

---

[3] Just before WWII ended, von Braun arranged the surrender of 500 top rocket scientists (including himself) to the Americans, along with the plans and experimental vehicles they'd been working on.

In 1904, Allen began working for A. P. Brink, the son of Washington Perry Brink who had founded the Chicago company in 1859. Allen was paid $5 a week to work from 7:00 a.m. to 7:00 p.m. six days a week, hauling all kinds of goods and freight in one of Brink's 200 horse-drawn wagons. When I photographed Allen it was exactly 50 years later and the one-time cartage driver was now chairman of the board of Brink's, Inc., a company that boasted "1,000 of the finest armored cars that money can buy" and 6,000 employees in 91 cities in the U.S. and Canada. The company was also moving and safeguarding $1 billion in cash each day. (Today Brink's is worldwide, is the largest armored transportation provider in America, has 246 branches, 2,228 armored vehicles and 9,214 employees.)

Allen ruefully talked about the $2.7 million Brink's robbery of 1950—which the press proclaimed "the crime of the century" and "the perfect crime"—but said that he was certain it would be solved. (It was, in late 1955, when one of the 10 gang members, "Specs" O'Keefe, confessed to the crime and ratted on his nine accomplices.)

Allen told us an interesting fact about Brink's truck holdups: most truck holdups are spur-of-the-moment. He said what happens is that some minor crook walking down the street sees a Brink's truck with the door open and the guards taking out bags of money. The crook just can't stand it. The adrenalin flows. He decides on the spot to stick up the truck. These spur-of-the-moment attempts, Allen added, usually fail.

Several years later, I was to photograph the top brass of the Federal Reserve Bank of Chicago for their annual report. Beforehand, I had to give security my license plate number and a description of my vehicle and was told to park my car at the loading dock in the bank.

When I came the next day, I was let in after my driver's license was checked. There were guards with shotguns in little glass-enclosed balconies above me and guards on the ground. I was directed to park at the far end of the loading dock which meant I had to pass a long line of armored Brink's trucks that were loading hundreds of bags of money.

I had a small handcart for my equipment that I loaded up. Now I know how those spur-of-the-moment crooks felt. If one of those crooks had been with me he would have had a heart attack. I had to walk past all these trucks and be careful not to be run over by carts of money. I thought if I left the tailgate down on my International Scout, maybe a bag of money would accidentally fall in. I knew that wouldn't happen but it was frustrating to be surrounded by mounds of money.

One banker said he told his tellers to think of the money as so many cans of beans. If they started thinking of it as money, they could be in trouble, he said. Well, anyway, the Federal Reserve shoot went well, and when I was finished I had to walk back through moneyland. Nobody left a bag in my car. But it wasn't a total loss. I was well paid by the bank.

Finance magazine never did exposés. The stories weren't puff pieces but the cover stories were always positive—which is one reason we were always welcome in the financial community. One of the best welcomes we received was the trip Tom Callahan—who replaced Sam Lyons as editor when Sam left—and I made to New Orleans to do a story on Eads Poitevent, ceo of International City Bank there.

(left) Eads Poitevent, ceo, International City Bank, New Orleans, LA, circa 1959

There is such a thing as southern hospitality. After a good interview Poitevent said, "I want to show you some of our projects." He drove us out to an empty field where a helicopter was waiting. That's a new way to see New Orleans. The cover photo was of Poitevent flying in the helicopter over New Orleans. He said, "Now, for dinner, you boys meet us at Antoine's Restaurant." I had been to New Orleans several times, and although the food was good, Antoine's wasn't my favorite restaurant. I thought it was sort of plain and didn't have much atmosphere.

When we met Poitevent and some of his top bank officers, we were ushered into a part of Antoine's I didn't know existed. It was a private dining room that seemed to be in a cave. It was lit like a movie set. Off to the side was another cave that was really a huge wine cellar with a large iron gate. I half-expected to see Count Dracula come out.

It was a terrific room. A large table was set up with all the glasses, silverware, and candles you would expect to see in a palace. We had a private bar and were served hors d'oeuvres. After many cocktails and good conversation with the friendly group, we sat down to eat. We looked around for the menu. "Now you boys just relax," said our host. "We took care of that." And the food started coming.

I don't remember everything we were served, there was so much, but even to this day I can say it was one of the best dinners I've ever eaten in my life. I know there were oysters, lobster, stuffed flounder, to begin. And steak. And for dessert they presented us with a large baked Alaska, the words "Welcome, Tom and George" written on it in icing. I always liked New Orleans, but I liked it more after that night.

Dwight Eisenhower. One time, while Eisenhower was president, I was in New York to photograph some bankers. I was having breakfast in my room at the Berkeley Hotel. Mohan liked the Berkeley so *Finance* usually stayed there. It was across the street from the Waldorf Astoria. I was watching the news on TV and saw President Eisenhower riding in a large, open car on his way to the Waldorf. When they showed his route, I realized he was only a couple of blocks away and would pass right under my window.

I grabbed my camera, opened the window, and saw him coming. I barely had time to focus—and there he was, standing up and waving. I got one shot and he was

Dean Witter, founder, Dean Witter & Co., San Francisco, CA, 1955

gone around the corner. The picture wasn't very good. There was some movement because of the car's speed. If I had had more time, I would have checked the shutter speed. Can you imagine me trying that today? I would probably be taken out by Secret Service bullets.

Dean Witter. In 1955, on one of our trips to San Francisco, Sam interviewed Dean Witter, famed founder of the investment banking firm bearing his name: Dean Witter & Co.

The man was one of those unbelievable American success stories *Finance* magazine avidly pursued. In 1914, at age 27, young Dean Witter and partner Charles Blyth, opened shop as investment bankers and brokers in San Francisco. Total capital? Ten thousand dollars. They named their firm Blyth, Witter & Co. Ten years later, the two men amicably parted to go out on their own. Witter's firm became Dean Witter & Co. He immediately hammered out a policy statement that served as his philosophy of business through the years:

"Let us try to stick to what we know is right. I think there is room for one firm on the Coast which is willing to subordinate profit to principles, that it should only handle business which is good, and should only do things which are right. I believe that the reward for such a firm will come not only in profit, but also in the more important medium of respect, which, once our physical needs are cared for, must be our major objective."

When Sam and I arrived at the Dean Witter headquarters in San Francisco in 1955, the company employed 800 people, had 28 offices all over the country and a net worth of $10.5 million.

Dean Witter came down to his office on a Saturday morning for the interview and photographs. At 68, he was a tall, handsome man with a great face to photograph. Just enough wrinkles to look good.

The interview and pictures went well. Witter told us how he had predicted the stock-market crash and the Great Depression that followed. While people were jumping out of windows in their desperation, the company came out very well financially. Dean Witter & Co. posted profits every year during the '30s and into the '40s.

Witter was also a great outdoorsman. At one point in the interview, he asked his secretary to call his ranch to get some information. She hesitated, then asked, "Which ranch?" What a life. Several years ago, an ad agency hired an actor to portray Dean Witter in its TV ads. The actor looked like an overweight couch potato. So much for the agency's research department.

By 1997, when Dean Witter Reynolds (Reynolds & Co. was an earlier acquisition) was bought by Morgan Stanley, it had annual revenues of $9.03 billion, total assets of $17.3 billion and 33,084 employees.

Witter's earliest partner and constant competitor through the years had done well too. Blyth & Co. had gone through a series of acquisitions and mergers, emerging as part of Paine Webber Co., which was acquired in 2000 by the Swiss-based UBS for $12 billion in cash.

President John F. Kennedy and Monroe Kimbrel, president of the American Bankers Association, Symposium of Economic Growth, Washington, D.C., 1963

John F. Kennedy. In February of 1963 the American Bankers Association held a symposium on economic growth at the Mayflower Hotel in Washington, D.C. The chairman of the event was David Rockefeller. The main speaker at the symposium was John F. Kennedy, president of the United States. I was there with Tom

President John F. Kennedy and David Rockefeller at Symposium of Economic Growth, Washington, D.C., 1963

Callahan, the editor of *Finance*. We had earlier told the ABA we would be there. Once at the Mayflower, Tom and I were given name tags, and that was it.

With only my name tag, I had no problem getting close to the president and shooting as many pictures as I wanted.

I was also able to photograph him in an anteroom before his speech. I was surprised how much better he looked in person. He was just up from Florida and he looked tan and rested and ready to take on this hostile group of bankers who didn't agree with his policies at all. I shot several more pictures while he gave his speech.

Afterward, he took questions from the audience, a group of 250 of the country's top minds in banking, industry, government, agriculture and labor. At the end of the program, they gave Kennedy a standing ovation.

At a reception after the program, I photographed most of the conference participants and the photo captions read like a list of Who's Who in the United States. Everyone seemed surprised—and happy—at how well the symposium went. (I also remember that the Mayflower Hotel had the best egg rolls.)

Many years later, I was to photograph former president Jimmy Carter, with a corporate CEO. The Secret Service not only called my home before the shoot, asking a few questions and wanting my social security number, but the day I photographed Carter the Secret Service arrived before he did and checked me and my equipment. Times sure had changed.

Betty Manning. While at *Finance,* Sam introduced me to Betty Manning, an old friend. Manning owned a very successful P.R. agency in New York. She bought one of those large old mansions on the upper East Side where all the foreign embassies are. I believe hers was built by the Remington typewriter people. Not only was it large, it was gorgeous. A bronze plaque mounted on it proclaimed "The Manning Building."

I liked Betty Manning. She was a tall, blond powerhouse. Most of the year, she wore a large, wide-brimmed mink hat that made it easy to find her in a crowd. Another reason I liked her was that she liked the pictures I did for *Finance* and hired me to do work for several of her clients.

Maybe one of the reasons she liked my photographs was that I always did my own darkroom work. I spent the time it takes to make good prints. If there was someone I especially liked who was baldheaded or had heavy shadows on his face, I would spend extra time burning in his head (making it darker so it wouldn't look like a light bulb) or working to hold back the shadows.

Manning was married to her partner, Jack Frost (his real name was Gardner Lane Frost). Jack was another powerhouse, and I enjoyed working with him, too. (He was bald and looked like a tall Erich von Stroheim, the silent film star/director.)

Jack loved New York. He liked to say you can get anything at any time in New York, if you have the money. You can get a haircut or a suit pressed at 3 a.m. He also liked to go to the best restaurants, slip the maitre d' a few bills, and get the best table.

The Manning Group liked to hang out at the nearby Carlisle Hotel bar. I think Betty brought in most of the business. Betty and Jack were quite a team. I remember talking to Jack about a shoot I had coming up for him. I told him what I had in mind to do. He said, "They all do that. I got you because I want something different!" That I liked. Many of my clients are afraid to do things differently. He was pleased with the results of the shoot.

I shot several stories for *Finance* that featured Manning clients. In fact, for years Betty Manning had been trying to buy the magazine from Mohan. But *Finance* was Mohan's life, and for a very long time she wouldn't budge. At last, after publishing the magazine for almost 20 years, Mohan finally gave in. I think she was just tired. A lot of her old banking friends were either dying or retiring. The fun was running out.

But Betty was very happy. She had big plans for *Finance*. Of course, she moved the headquarters from the Chicago Opera House to the Manning Building in New York. It was a sad day but I didn't feel too bad. I had also felt the fun was running out. For a time, with Sam and Vern in the Opera House and Don and Nick across the street in the Hearst building, I practically lived off that corner of Madison Street and Wacker Drive. I will always have a very soft spot in my heart for the Opera House.

Tom would leave eventually and I would still do some stories for the magazine and for Manning's agency, but I knew it would never be the same. One of the first things Betty did after buying the magazine was to hire the famous photographer, Yousuf Karsh, to shoot the covers. *In color.* That was a first for *Finance*. She invited Tom and me over for cocktails one night at the Manning Building. Besides the office, Jack and Betty had a beautiful apartment in the mansion. She also invited Karsh. We could all talk about the future magazine.

I was happy to meet Karsh, the living legend. There is no doubt that for the kind of work he did he was the best. I looked forward to hearing stories of some of the famous people he'd shot. However, he wasn't a storyteller. He wasn't very humble either. I asked who had hired him for a certain picture I had seen in a recent magazine. He replied, "You hire a horse, you don't hire Karsh!" He wasn't very warm, but he certainly was arrogant. That's O.K. If you've got it, flaunt it. He was still a great photographer. And I thought it would be a plus for me to tell people I was replaced by Karsh.

After many, many cocktails, I think Betty cooked something. I remember loud discussions, but don't remember if anything was accomplished. In time, Betty changed the look of the magazine and, without Mohan, the style. I did less and less work for her. Tom Callahan accepted a great job as P.R. director of Swift & Co. I forget the timing, but it was just a few years until Betty was diagnosed with cancer and died too young.

And that was the end of the magazine. *Finance* had been a huge and wonderful part of my life, especially the early years with Sam.

Flame-thrower, basic training, Fort Dix, New Jersey, 1951

Chapter Seven

Disaster

On June 25, 1950, when North Korea crossed the 38th parallel and invaded South Korea, President Harry Truman and the United Nations swung into action. Though it was called a U.N. "police action," the defense of South Korea was led by the United States with the president reinstituting the draft. Not a popular decision.

Since, however, I had fulfilled my service obligation in the Merchant Marines during WWII, I felt sure I wouldn't be drafted.

So 1950 started out as a very good year for me. I had a new wife, a new car, and a new apartment overlooking Lake Michigan. My photography business was good and growing. But overnight my life changed. President Truman decided that Merchant Marine service during WWII didn't count any longer; he would draft all the seamen young enough to fight in the Korean conflict. The Truman administration never called Korea a war, even though 1,751,820 American troops served in Korea and 33,629 of them died there.

I soon became 1-A so that I could be drafted before my upcoming twenty-sixth birthday. As JFK would later say, "Life ain't fair." I was devastated. I appealed, but to no avail. Several months later I was in the Army, which meant I gave up my car, my business, and moved my wife to a cheaper apartment.

I was sent to Fort Leonard Wood, Missouri, for basic training. It was a nightmare training with a bunch of 18-year-olds, many of whom thought it was fun to march and shoot guns. I didn't volunteer for anything, got through basic training, and was shipped to Mineral Wells, Texas, to Wolters Air Force Base.

Wolters was an Air Force base without airplanes. It didn't make sense, until I learned it was run by the Air Force as a training camp for Army engineers who specialize in building airstrips. It was called an Aviation Engineer Battalion, 472 AEB.

Again, I didn't volunteer for anything. But someone must have looked in my file and noticed that I was a photographer. So they sent me to photo school at the Army Signal Corps Photographic Center in Ft. Monmouth, New Jersey. It was one of the few pleasant surprises I had in the Army.

Fort Monmouth was a country club compared to Wolters AFB. I was assigned to a class of about 10 guys from various outfits around the country. Our instructor was a sergeant about my age and a very pleasant guy. The whole class was of a somewhat higher caliber than the group in Texas.

I didn't mind that I already knew about 90 percent of what the instructor was teaching. Mostly we used Speed Graphics so, for me, it was a holiday. I would bug the sergeant once in a while when he made a mistake, but in general I went along. The food was much better than in Texas. When the weather was good we ate outside at picnic tables, the barracks were decent, and most of the people were nice. I even made a few friends. But I was still in the Army.

The best part was going on field trips. Fort Monmouth is situated in a very beautiful area that includes the shore points—Red Bank, Asbury Park and Princeton. We would go out for the day and take pictures in one area, like Asbury Park, come back and develop the film, make prints and the next day our instructor would critique them. For me, the class wasn't a challenge. Plus, I was pretty popular with the other guys because they knew that, if they had a problem regarding the pictures, I would help them.

One such field trip was to the campus of Princeton University, another beautiful location. A student stopped to ask me what all the Army people were doing there. I told him we were photographing the buildings because the Army was going to take them over and make barracks out of them. He turned pale and walked away.

Another nonscientific field trip was to Fort Dix to photograph soldiers in basic training. I thought most of New Jersey was a beautiful state, but definitely not this part of it. Here it was cold, raining and muddy. The soldiers were sleeping in pup tents, and no one looked happy. We photographed tanks, troops and flame-throwers.

I guess it made more sense for us to photograph troops in action than to take pictures of the merry-go-round in Asbury Park. The photo class lasted a few months; then it was back to Mineral Wells.

One day I got a message to report to battalion headquarters. Now what? I was met there by the battalion's top sergeant whose name was Nicolas Nicaten. He was the spitting image of Burt Lancaster in *"From Here To Eternity,"* over six feet tall and handsome. A perfect physical specimen. His uniform was spotless. He was soft-spoken and looked like a recruiting poster for the Army. My file was on his desk. What did he want with me?

He walked me over to another room and opened the door to a beautiful, fully equipped darkroom with a Speed Graphic sitting on a table. "Do you know how to work all this stuff?" he asked. "Yes," I murmured.

Then he sat me down and interviwed me about my background. He was impressed. He also knew from my file that I was not the best soldier in the Army. He said, "The battalion is authorized one still photographer. You want to give it a try? You do good and I'll take care of you." I said, "Sure." I was beginning to like this guy.

I later found out that, like Burt Lancaster in *"From Here to Eternity,"* he pretty much ran the battalion. For openers he said, "Forget your company. When you get up in the morning you come here."

By now it was early 1953, and I had given up hope of getting any kind of early discharge. This would be a hell of a lot better than doing KP all the time. I started the next day. The Air Force had its own photo setup that included a well-equipped studio, and I would have access to that. The Army engineers had an array of heavy equipment: Caterpillar tractors, huge cranes, graders, steamrollers, and much more.

My job was to shoot progress reports, training brochures, head shots and anything else that came up. Sergeant Nicaten had said if I did a good job and made him look good, life would be better for me. True to his word, I soon had better living quarters and my own jeep; all of his reports became beautifully illustrated. He was happy with my work, and we soon became good friends: the private and the master sergeant. He was the best person I met in the Army.

Life did become better when I had my own niche. If formal portraits were needed I could go over to the Air Force and use their studio. People started coming to me for favors. *That* was a switch.

One Air Force sergeant I knew asked me to develop some pictures he had taken of his girlfriend that he didn't want to take to the drugstore for developing. No problem. He owned a Piper Cub airplane that he kept in a nearby field. He took me up whenever I needed to make aerial pictures. I learned if you want anything done in the Army, only deal with sergeants. They run the place.

One day, we got word that a terrible tornado had hit Waco, Texas. More than 100 people were killed, and the city was devastated. Much of the battalion was ordered to pack up the heavy equipment and leave immediately for Waco, about sixty or seventy miles away.

Soon a large convoy of tractors, bulldozers, cranes, many trucks, and other heavy equipment was on the road heading south. Waco was a mess. Blocks of buildings were demolished. Cars were in trees. A department store was destroyed. It had been five or six stories high and its floors had pancaked on top of each other. All that was left was a huge pile of rubble.

It was sad to see the local undertaker pulling out the bodies of people he knew. I stayed there for a few days photographing the engineers cleaning up the horrible mess. Anyone who lived in Waco at that time will never forget it. When we got back, Sergeant Nicaten put out an illustrated report on the excellent job the engineers had done in Waco.

I spent the rest of my Army time in Mineral Wells trying to keep out of trouble, just getting along. And one day the order came down. My time was up. I was finally being honorably discharged. I left for Chicago the same day I was discharged and never looked back. It was November 13, 1953.

No one can say I'm not a good American, but what really hurt about the Korean conflict—and later the Vietnam war—was that too many politicians and sons of politicians and well-connected people found a way to beat the draft. It hurt even more when, in 1988, 43 years after WWII, Congress passed a law giving WWII Merchant Marine veterans full-fledged veteran status with benefits. It was a little late, though, to take advantage of the G.I. Bill.

By the time I got back to Chicago things had changed radically. International News Photos (INP) had gone out of business. Don Alford had gone into the insurance business, Charlie Nickels had gone to work for a Los Angeles newspaper and would later become chief photographer at Disneyland. And Vern Whaley's son and daughter were now old enough to run Photo Ideas. I would still get some work from them but not much. All the public relations people I knew were using other photographers. Carl Snyder was about to leave Cuneo to start a business manufacturing satin sheets. That later turned into a profitable account for me, but for the present, the only clients ready to take me back were Sam and Mohan at *Finance* magazine. They were lifesavers.

I was broke and worked out of my apartment. I activated the old darkroom in my mother's basement that I had used when I was in high school. It wasn't much, but it worked for a while. It would take time to work my way back to where I was before I went into the Army.

Gradually, I did pick up more work. In less than a year I was able to rent a small studio and darkroom at Clark and Division Streets in Chicago. The next year, things really started to get better—that is, for work but not at home. For the next few years I was involved in a long, bitter, and very expensive divorce, which is why I was living with my old friend, Bob Kotalik.

After the Army, things were never the same. But unlike the 33,629 Americans who died in Korea, I was lucky. I could get on with the rest of my life.

Prudential Building, Chicago, IL, under construction, circa 1954

CHAPTER EIGHT

Better Times

Thank God for good friends. As I said before, Don Alford was now selling insurance for Prudential. I don't think he needed the money. Although he was in his 70s, he was still a ball of fire and just wasn't the type to retire. His son was a big producer at Prudential so Don became a Prudential agent too. And from time to time he would call me to see how I was doing.

One day he called to tell me to see Harry Adel at Prudential's Chicago headquarters. Prudential was then operating out of a huge warehouse on Canal Street. I said, "OK." To be truthful, it didn't sound like much to me. What's to shoot? A bunch of insurance people in warehouse offices?

Don called a few days later to ask how I did. I said I hadn't gotten around to it yet. He said, "Listen, sweetheart, they're reorganizing the company and are going to build the tallest building in Chicago. They're going to need plenty of pictures. Get the hell over there!" I felt like a real jerk.

The next day I went to see Harry Adel, in charge of advertising and P.R. for Prudential. He reminded me of Groucho Marx, with a smaller mustache. His favorite expression was "Christ, babe," as in "Christ, babe, that sounds good!" or "Christ, babe, we can't do that."

I showed him my portfolio and he said, "Christ, babe, that looks good. We'll give you a try."

There wasn't much work at first but after the groundbreaking the new Prudential Building became almost a full-time job for me. It would be the first skyscraper built in Chicago since the Great Depression. I don't know of another building that received as much publicity.

The best part of the project was the people. Along with Harry, Dan Becker and Frank Roberts were brought in from the Newark headquarters. Dan was the top sergeant. A tall, curly-headed guy who looked very much the executive, Dan ran the advertising and P.R. department day to day. He had such a dry sense of humor, I doubted he would be much fun to work with. Was I wrong.

Frank was the art director, a stocky, dark-haired guy who could pass for one of the Sopranos of the popular TV series. There would be no problem working with him.

Tall, lean, long-haired Van Beverly, the very talented artist, was from Chicago. Also from Chicago were Art Hrobsky, Dick Westerveldt and Jerry Wherity. Art looked like a college professor and did most of the writing. His favorite expression was "You betcha," as in "Can we do this, Art?" "You betcha." An affable guy, he usually didn't attend the long lunches and parties that often took place with the rest of the department.

Dick was good at marketing and handled much of it. He looked like a cherub with glasses and had a great sense of humor. Jerry was the youngest of the group and the least experienced, but he quickly mastered his job and became a real asset to the department.

I later met the senior vice-president, James E. Rutherford, who headed the entire Mid-America home office construction project. "Big Jim" was from Newark and he was sharp. Everyone liked him. He talked like a good ol' boy from Tennessee or Kentucky but no one ever put anything over on him. He knew all that went on and how to fix any problem. He was responsible for most of the success of the Mid-America project.

These men were not nine-to-fivers. If a project needed to be done fast it was, no matter if it meant staying late or coming in early.

U.S. Steel South Works, circa 1954

After ground was broken, I had plenty of work from Prudential, shooting almost every phase of the building's construction. Then I looked up Tom Ward. I had met him while I was working for INP and he had just begun working in the P.R. department for U.S. Steel Corporation. Seemed that U.S. Steel's American Bridge Division was putting up the steel work of the Prudential Building. Tom hired me to make progress pictures as the building went up. So every time a few more floors were added, I would go out to Grant Park and shoot a picture from the same location to show the progress. I also shot many photos of the mills at U.S. Steel plus other P.R. events.

Before one shoot, Tom stopped to pick up something at his parents' apartment on Lake Shore Drive. I went with him and was surprised to see the apartment walls covered with autographed pictures of famous sports figures.

I said to Tom, "Your father must really like sports." "Um," said Tom. I later learned that Arch Ward, the famous *Chicago Tribune* sports columnist was his father. Tom must have figured out I wasn't much of a sports fan. But in spite of that, he was fun to work with and we got along well.

I was now working for the Prudential Company and U.S. Steel. When Otis Elevator Company, due to install the world's fastest elevators in the building, needed a photographer, my friends recommended me. Thus Otis also became my client. As far as I was concerned, Prudential could have been named the Bread and Butter Building.

As the building went up, I spent a lot of time crawling around on top of the steel structure with a 4x5 camera. The Prudential was built with millions of red-hot steel rivets for one reason: they provided the strongest joints.[1] That meant I had to be careful not to get hit with one of those red-hot rivets as it was tossed from the "heater man" at the fire to the "catch man" who caught it in a bucket a few yards away.

It was amazing to see those steel workers walking on narrow beams 30 or 40 stories high with no protection.

I was up there on the Prudential beams too, but I always crawled. I did get great pictures, but I admit that many times I was really scared. Like the time I walked

---

[1] The glowing red-hot rivet is fed through precisely drilled holes in the steel beam. The unformed end of the rivet is quickly hammered to close the joint. When the rivet cools, it contracts to squeeze the joint tightly together.

Top to bottom; Prudential Building under construction, circa 1954; Heating rivets to red-hot

"Topping out" ceremony of the Prudential Building, 1954

down the stairway from the twentieth floor. As I turned the corner, the stairway ended with nothing beneath me! At times, making construction photos of that building was harrowing, but mostly it was great fun.

When the building was "topped out" in 1954, the Governor of Illinois William ("Billy the Kid") Stratton, Mayor Martin Kennelley of Chicago, and all the top people at Prudential and U.S. Steel attended, as well as local politicians and the media.

The Prudential Building was 41 stories high when it was finished. At 601 feet (912' with its antenna spire) it was the tallest building in Chicago until 1969 when the John Hancock Center was built. ("Big John" is 1,127 feet and 100 stories high.)

The building was an immediate, tremendous success. Chicago's expanding Leo Burnett advertising agency was one of its charter tenants, having outgrown its 11 floors of the London Guarantee Building, at the SW corner of Michigan Avenue and Wacker Drive.

Though Leo Burnett himself had initially balked at the Prudential's 20-year lease, three factors closed the deal: Leo's new office would be on the 15th floor (the same as it was in the London Guarantee Building), he could keep the company's

The completed Prudential Building, 1957

Lobby, Prudential Building, 1957

old phone number (Central 6-5959) and best of all, his new office would have a private washroom.

Celebrities passing through Chicago insisted on visiting the Prudential's Observation Deck, which surrounded the Top of the Rock restaurant and bar on the 41st floor. Two of the early visitors were 17-year old Natalie Wood and her co-star, 24-year old Tab Hunter, in town to publicize their new film, *"The Girl He Left Behind."*

Whether tenants or employees, everyone wanted to work in the new Prudential Building. I met more than one person in the lobby looking for any job as long as it was in the Prudential.

One reason it was so popular is that the building was just plain fun, especially the top floor. But I spent more time on the ground floor, next door at Randy's, a friendly, less formal restaurant/bar, where it was unlikely you'd run into your boss. Whenever we needed to find someone from the advertising and P.R. department, the first place to look was Randy's.

The work was always done. If you had a break, however, it made more sense to go to Randy's than to sit in your office looking busy. I remember spending most of one afternoon in Randy's while Van Beverly explained Cubism to me.

I spent about three years working with Prudential, from construction of the new building to when the company moved in.

Once the building was fully occupied and the novelty wore off, there wasn't as much work for me. I still photographed the bigger conferences and special events, but construction of the new building had been the main event. After the dust settled, many in the advertising and P.R. department left for greener pastures.

Dan Becker left to run the new home office which Prudential was building in Boston. A couple of years later, when I was in Boston I called him. Dan was now one of the top executives with Prudential. I said, "Can we have lunch?" He replied that he was very busy but maybe a quick one. I said fine, I have to catch a plane later and can't take much time either.

I met Dan at a very fine restaurant and we started to talk about and drink to Chicago. I missed my plane and he never went back to his office that day.

Natalie Wood and Tab Hunter on the Observation Deck, Prudential Building, circa 1957

Dick Westerveldt left for New York to join marketing whiz Stanley Arnold's successful firm. He later brought Jerry Wherity to work with him. Not much later Jerry married his English secretary and moved to London where he started a successful marketing business with Frank Roberts. I visited Jerry a couple of years later in London. He sent the company Rolls Royce and chauffeur to pick me up at the airport.

Van Beverly went off to Spain for a year to paint. When he returned to Chicago he had a very successful gallery show, then moved to New York and enjoyed a dual career as a fine artist and also as an artist for NBC's nightly newscast, the *"Huntley-Brinkley Report."* Art Hrobsky also left Prudential but stayed in Chicago to pursue a successful writing career.

The Prudential's advertising and P.R. department was the best group of people I've ever worked with.

Carl Byoir & Associates, one of the many top P.R. firms in the country I worked for, was my second favorite group of people, for two reasons. Byoir had great accounts: RCA, B.F. Goodrich, Chemetron Corp., Cargill Grain and, at one time, even had Howard Hughes as a client. The second reason I liked working for Byoir was Hank McAlister.

Hank was in charge of all the photography for Byoir. He was a genuine New Yorker, accent and all. When I see Bill O'Reilly I'm reminded of Hank. Same style of talking. One day, out of the blue, Hank called me from New York for a small job in Chicago. The job went well. Hank said he would be in touch with me and there would be more work.

During the next few years we would travel all over the country doing feature stories about Byoir's clients that he would then place in magazines and newspapers. We also did photography for many annual reports. His assignments were always fun.

One of the most intriguing shoots was at the government's U.S. National Atomic Reactor Testing Station in Idaho Falls, Idaho. I've never been as impressed with security before or since. After we entered the Reactor Testing Station through double gates, guards went through my photo equipment and wrote down all the serial numbers of my cameras and lenses to be checked again when we left. I can only guess at the secret operations that were going on there.

My job was to photograph a tire. B.F. Goodrich scientists were experimenting with a new way to vulcanize tires. We were led into a room that held what looked like a large swimming pool. Bright violet rods glowed in the water. We met the scientist who explained that a metal tire mold with a raw tire in it had been placed into the pool and was "cooking" in the atomic water to see if it would vulcanize into a finished tire.

The atmosphere was nervous. In some areas we had to wear special shoes. I photographed the pool and the tire mold that was in the water. I also walked on a plank set over the pool to shoot at a better angle. I was too young and dumb to realize that if I fell into the pool I would be cooked too.

The tire had been in the pool for several days and we were there for the opening of the mold to see if the experiment worked. When the mold was opened, out came a beautiful tire. Everyone was thrilled. I took more pictures and then we all left for the airport.

It was fun to see the scientist on the plane sitting next to his tire that he bought a seat for. He wasn't about to let it out of his sight.

Another interesting job had to do with pigs. Hank called me one day and said to meet him at a small motel in northern Wisconsin. That was his style. He told you where and when to be somewhere; how you did it was up to you. I had to look on a map to find the town and ended up driving there.

When I arrived Hank explained the story. A local farmer had invented a new kind of pigpen. It seems that when a sow nurses its piglets, she often rolls over on her babies and can kill one or two. This new pigpen was round and had a kind of railing in the center that prevented the sow from rolling over on her piglets.

Byoir had worked out a promotion with one of its animal food clients to promote the new pigpen and Hank had brought a movie photographer with him from New York to shoot film to give to the TV news stations.

Out on the farm there were only the three of us and the farmer. I had the movie cameraman hold a clip-board of papers to look like a farm expert discussing the pigpen with the farmer. After I got my shots we reversed roles and I became the "expert." Anyone who knew me and saw that film had a big laugh.

Another time we were in St. Louis to shoot the loading of corn onto huge barges for Cargill. We agreed that the best shot would be from the bottom of the barge, looking up as the corn poured in from a very large hose.

I climbed down a ladder to the bottom of the barge and Hank lowered the camera. When I was ready they turned on the corn. It made a great picture. Thank God, they turned off the corn when it was up to my waist. I thought I shook all the corn out of my clothes, but on the plane back to Chicago I left a trail of corn every time I moved. I'm sure the other passengers wondered about me.

When National Cylinder Gas was planning to rename its different divisions under one new name, it was a well-guarded secret. Though I made photographs at some of the divisions that would be renamed when the name change was announced to the press, Hank never told me that this was about to happen.

I learned about it one day when I went to Louisville, Kentucky, to take pictures at one of the divisions called Tube Turns, which made elbows for pipelines and other industrial uses. Earlier I had mentioned to Mohan Louis, the publisher of *Finance* Magazine, that I would be in Louisville the following week and had some spare time. Did she have some banker she wanted photographed? (I was always looking to make an extra buck.) She did and made arrangements for me to shoot the chairman of the biggest bank in Louisville.

So when I got a break at Tube Turns I ran over to the bank to shoot the chairman. His name was Earl and he was a real Southerner. He said, "What are you-all doing in town?" I told him I was taking pictures at Tube Turns. He said he was a director of that company and asked if I knew they were going to change the name to Chemetron Corporation.

When I got back to the factory I told Hank the news. "Goddammit, who the hell told you that?" he yelled. When I told him, he wasn't about to bawl out a director of the company. I promised I wouldn't tell anyone.

One year, when RCA held its annual meeting in Chicago at the Civic Opera House, Hank hired me to photograph the meeting and also to follow around and photograph the ceo, David Sarnoff, for the day.

After the annual meeting Sarnoff left for a small meeting at a regional office and suddenly everything became a big deal. His staff constantly referred to him as General. Not the General. It was just General. General wants this, or General wants that. Everyone seemed afraid of him but I thought he was an arrogant little man and didn't much care for him. Nothing I would tell Hank, however.

Byoir had a Chicago office. I never contacted them and Hank said it was just as well, they didn't have much going on. I think he wanted me exclusively. But one day Dick Davis, the manager of Carl Byoir's Chicago office, called me for a job. Remember, I am a child of the Great Depression and never said no to work. As it turned out, the Chicago office had more work than I expected.

Dick was an unusual guy. At one time he did P.R. for Howard Hughes and had photographs in his office of the two of them together. He revered Hughes. He was also one of the few people who flew in Hughes' massive airplane, the all-wooden "Spruce Goose" on its only flight: one minute at an altitude of 70 feet on November 2, 1947.

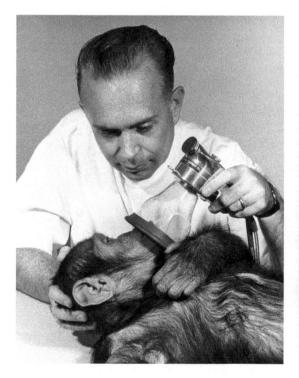 

Left to right; Demonstrating oxygen mask made for animals by National Cylinder Gas, 1963; Experiment with liquid oxygen on flowers, circa 1964

Dick introduced me to Walter Coyne, a new employee I would be working with. Walter was a New Yorker from a well-to-do family and a graduate of Holy Cross College in Indiana. To this day, I don't know what we had in common but for some reason we connected extremely well. Maybe it was because he was the spitting image of Bob Newhart and had a great sense of humor. Plus we always had assignments that brought out the fun.

Like the National Cylinder Gas' custom-designed oxygen masks for both animals and humans. For one assignment, we used a very clever chimp who not only posed obligingly as the "patient" being resuscitated with oxygen but who thoroughly examined and carefully handled each piece of the equipment.

Walter also set up some surprising experiments using liquid oxygen to freeze flowers, which I photographed the moment they exploded. To what end, I never knew. There was never a dull moment on Chemetron shoots.

Walter had been recently married and didn't know many people in Chicago. After getting to know him a little better I invited him and his wife, Joyce, to dinner. My wife, Joan, and Joyce got along famously. For one thing, they were both bookworms. We four soon became close friends.

When I was renovating an old building in Old Town into a studio and living quarters, Joyce and Joan spent months stripping a hundred years of paint off the giant doors in the studio. The doors came out beautifully and made a great background for many fashion photos.

A few years later Walter took a better job in Washington, D.C.—writing speeches for President Lyndon Johnson in the White House. And, after a couple of years in Washington, Walter and Joyce moved to Los Angeles where Walter became executive speechwriter with the Atlantic Richfield Company where he remained 24 years until he retired. We remained close friends until 2008, when he died too young.

I repeat. Thank God for good friends.

Wells St. studio doors after restoration, 1965

Lena Horne, Chicago, 1955

CHAPTER NINE

El Dorado

After WWII until the early 1970s, Chicago was truly the golden city of entertainment. I was lucky to live in Chicago at a time when, if you went to see an act or show, you actually saw the performers up close in an intimate environment. That's why today I will not go to a show or concert in a stadium, football field, or monster auditorium where a giant screen and hundreds of speakers are necessary to see and hear what those little specks on stage are doing.

It was an incredible time. Chicago was bursting with talent, and I got to see most of it and photograph much of it. Because I knew and worked with many of the P.R. people who handled the entertainers, it was easy for me to get into a place even if it were sold out. Vern Whaley, through the *Chicago Herald American,* could always get me theater tickets for the shows that came through town. Here are just some of the places and entertainers I loved that made Chicago so exciting then.

Among the people you could see at Mister Kelly's on Rush Street were comedians Woody Allen, Mort Sahl, or Phyllis Diller doing stand-up routines. Phyllis bragged that she wore hats by the popular and expensive hat designer John Frederics but, in her early days, I think it was a huge investment for her. You could also hear Barbra Streisand, who was just beginning to make her reputation, sing at Mister Kelly's.

The London House, in the London Guarantee Building on the corner of Wacker Drive and Michigan Avenue, was owned by the same Marienthal brothers who owned Mister Kelly's. Although it was an outstanding restaurant for both lunch and dinner, in the evening the London House featured great musicians performing.

I photographed Jonah Jones and his swinging quartet there. Jones had started playing jazz trumpet as an 11-year-old. His first professional gig was aboard a sternwheeler riverboat on the Mississippi River. Later, he played with jazz greats Jimmie Lunceford, Fletcher Henderson, Benny Carter, and he was with Cab Calloway for 11 years. When Calloway's orchestra was signed to play in the original production of *"Porgy and Bess,"* Jones was lead trumpet. (He also had a bit part in the play.)

Later, Jonah Jones and his quartet recorded steadily in the 1950s and 1960s with Capitol and Decca. His *"I Dig Chicks"* album was a Grammy winner in 1958 and several of his singles sold over a million copies each.

The Chez Paree on Banks Court was one of the most popular nightclubs in Chicago's history. The biggest stars from all over the country entertained there and I photographed several of them—Jimmy Durante, Danny Thomas, Herb Shriner, Sophie Tucker.

Jimmy Durante, Chicago, 1964

One of my favorite pictures of all time is one I took of Lena Horne when she appeared at the Chez. I shot her in her dressing room while she was being interviewed for a magazine story.

Her hair was in curlers. She was wearing a chenille bathrobe and a pair of huge diamond earrings. I couldn't believe she would let me shoot her that way, but she did. I got an amazing close-up of her with her little Pug dog. I have never met another entertainer, male or female, who had the confidence to let me shoot them dressed like that. I think it was impossible to take a bad picture of Lena Horne. And of all the pictures I've shot, this one is my favorite.

I went to the Chez often, usually to photograph some celebrity being interviewed by Mike Wallace and his then wife, Buff Cobb, who were doing their radio show from the Chez Paree VIP Lounge. I remember Lucille Ball marching in one night for an interview with her husband, Desi Arnaz. Lucy did all the talking and gave all the orders. There was no doubt who was the boss.

I was surprised the night I saw Liberace perform. I hadn't realized he played the piano that well. And after her performances Sophie Tucker would sit in the lobby, autographing and selling records for one of the many charities in which she was interested.

One night I met a man in the Lounge who said he was throwing a birthday party for Sophie Tucker the next week and would I take a picture of the group? Of course I would. I went to his downtown apartment and shot a group picture and made prints for everyone in the picture. I sent him a bill and never heard from him again. After a few phone calls I gave up. The crook never paid me. I was lucky at that. During my entire career, this was one of only two times I didn't get paid for a job.

One time at the Opera House I was photographing a French opera star when the name of the Chez Paree came up. The opera singer asked if the Chez Paree was fran-caise. Danny Newman, the P.R. man for the Lyric Opera, replied, "No, it is he-brew."

The Chez had a chorus line known as the Chez Paree Adorables. (And they were.) One summer I was doing publicity pictures for the harness track in Maywood

Park. Ernie Simon, the host of a popular local TV show, was there with Sid Caesar, whom I was to photograph. Suddenly, an announcement came over the loud speaker. "Honored guests tonight are Ernie Simon, Sid Caesar and a 28-year-old Chez Paree Adorable."

I thought that was pretty funny and so did they.

S.R.O. was a small club on North Clark Street near North Avenue. I went there often to hear a young jazz pianist, Ramsey Lewis, and his trio. I knew he had a great career ahead of him.

Today, three-time Grammy winner Lewis continues to record, perform live and tour. He hosts the two-hour *"Legends of Jazz with Ramsey Lewis"* on 65 radio stations every week. He's artistic director of Ravinia Festival's *"Jazz at Ravinia"* Series and was the organizer of its Jazz Mentor Program in Chicago's high schools. During his long career he's appeared with over 25 symphony orchestras in the U.S. and Canada and has appeared in music festivals in Europe, Japan and Mexico.

Jazz Ltd. on East Grand Avenue was created by clarinet player Bill Reinhardt, whose joy was Dixieland jazz. He and his wife Ruth, a beautiful, exotic Chinese-American, started a jazz club on the ground floor of an old brownstone, a lot like the places on 52nd Street in New York City. Bill played the music and Ruth ran the club as manager, maitre'd and bookkeeper. The exhilarating band featured Bill, and the place caught on quickly. When *Time* magazine did a story, Jazz Ltd. *really* took off and was standing room only for several years.

The Blue Note was downtown in the Loop in the lower level of an office building on Madison Street. It featured top bands like Louis Armstrong's and up-and-coming stars like a young, beautiful Sarah Vaughan. At the time, Dave Garroway had a radio show and was always raving about the Blue Note on the air. Some people thought he had a financial interest in the club, but whether he did or didn't, the Blue Note's jazz was always the best.

One night Mel Tormé was performing there and I was sitting at a table upfront with Mel's friends, Sarah Vaughan and Dick La Palm, the local P.R. man for Mel's agent. It had been a long day, it was late, and I was dozing off. In the middle of one of his songs, Mel hollered down, "Wake up, George." We all laughed. I stayed awake.

The Empire Room at the Palmer House was one of the most elegant rooms in town, always showcasing the best entertainers. I photographed some of them. When I wasn't working, I could always get a good table from my friend Freddie Townsend, the P.R. man there. I paid my own way to a sold-out performance of the great French singer, Edith Piaf. The orchestra played behind a translucent curtain and Piaf was on the stage alone, wearing an ordinary blue dress. Her performance was extraordinary and worth every penny I paid.

Second City had its beginnings in 1959 in a former Chinese laundry at the junction of Clark, Lincoln, and Wells Streets. It was an immediate success because the troupe was hilarious.

Forty-six years later, Second City is still going strong in a much larger theater on Wells Street, but I think its first few years were the best. All I remember about Alan Arkin and Barbara Harris doing an hysterical skit in an art museum was that I fell off the chair laughing.

Eugene Troobnick did a takeoff on Superman. When the country was in financial trouble, he would go into a phone booth and come out dressed as Business Man. In his business suit and carrying an attaché case he could throw up tariff walls and move the stock market up.

Another favorite skit was Paul Sand as a Vietnamese farmer. An American adviser gives him a bayonet. The farmer implies it will be helpful in planting his crops. The advisor says, "No, you stupid savage, it's not for farming, it's for killing!"

The Walton Walk was one of the first key clubs in Chicago. You didn't get a key, you got a card that you put in a slot in the door and then the man inside opened the door. It was located just off Walton and Rush Streets. Small, intimate, elegant, the Walton Walk was owned by Arnold Morton.

Morton hired Victor Lownes III, who had no publicity experience, to do his P.R. Victor did such a terrific job for the club, which included inventing the famous Mortinee (his version of the martini named after Morton), that a short time later he and Arnold were both hired by Hugh Hefner and became top executives with *Playboy*.

The Italian Village is made up of three restaurants on Monroe Street, between Clark and Dearborn. It occupies a two-story building and basement, with a different style restaurant on each floor, all of them excellent. Still run by the Capitanini family, as it has been since 1927, the Italian Village doesn't offer entertainment but does host many of the best parties for entertainers I've ever been to, all held there in the lower-level restaurant called La Cantina. My friend Bob Howe was the P.R. man for the Italian Village, and he had me shoot many of the festivities.

My favorite parties were given each November at La Cantina by the cast from the Lyric Opera. They were held to celebrate the birthday of Tito Gobbi, one of opera's greatest baritones. After the performance on his birthday, the cast would throw a great party for him at La Cantina.

I love opera singers. They always seem to be so alive and happy. I also loved watching them eat. Platters of Rock Cornish hens were passed around like popcorn. (This was after a performance.) Carol Fox, the dynamic founder of the Lyric Opera, would always be there too.

At the time, Charles Gilbert was general manager of the Civic Opera House. He and his wife were friends of my parents, which meant I got to see most of the attractions at the Opera House. Mr. Gilbert didn't always agree with Carol Fox and said she sometimes could be very demanding. As an example, he recounted the time she wanted the curtain of what was then probably the largest stage in Chicago to be taken down and washed. Mr. Gilbert thought it was a huge, expensive, and unnecessary project. Carol Fox prevailed.

One of the wonderful parties at La Cantina was given by playwright/producer Moss Hart for Ann Rogers and the entire cast of *"My Fair Lady"* on its one-hundredth Chicago performance.

Club DeLisa, in the heart of the black community at State Street and Garfield Boulevard, was what they used to call a black-and-tan club where everyone—blacks and whites—were welcome. It was a huge place (with the smallest tables), fantastic entertainment, and featured the great Red Saunders orchestra. Big-name performers like Count Basie and Joe Williams appeared there. One of my favorites was Peg Leg Bates, a one-legged tap dancer you had to see to believe.

*(l-r) Ray Capitanini
and Moss Hart,
circa 1955*

The tiny round tables had very heavy cast-iron bases. I loved to see one of the giant-sized employees pick up a table with one hand and move it around like a toy. Such immense presences kept everybody in line. Many nights, I parked my car two blocks away and would come out of the Club DeLisa at two in the morning and walk to my car with no problem. I miss Chicago's south side of the '50s.

There were too many other fantastic nightspots in Chicago to mention, and I know I tried to hit them all. It was a magical time to be here.

Wilhelmina, Chicago, 1960

CHAPTER TEN

No Ordinary People

Some of the men and women I met and worked with I knew for only a short time. Others have remained friends for life. I've already written here of many of them, but I'm adding another group: unforgettable people I was thrilled to know.

Wilhelmina, aka Gertrude W. Behmenburg. In 1959 I was shooting pictures for my friend Carl Snyder, the former P.R. man for Hawthorn Mellody, who was now in the business of manufacturing satin bedsheets. The photos were for national magazine ads and were to be very respectable.

I needed a glamorous model to pose in bed with the sheets draped around her, showing some skin but not too much. Unlike today, models then were not anxious to show much skin. If they did, they wanted to wear body stockings and be paid double their rate. And if they heard the words satin sheets, bed, and skin, they got *really* nervous.

I thought I had the solution. I would book a nude model and be able to drape the sheets any way I needed to. Now to find a glamorous, sophisticated nude model.

I called my friend Sabie, who ran Sabie's Models Unlimited, a modeling school and agency on Wabash Avenue in Chicago's Loop. His agency wasn't known for fashion models but more for publicity and cheesecake. Sabie's wife, however, was Ann Marsters, the movie critic for the *Chicago Herald American,* a Hearst paper. She constantly dealt with movie stars. Maybe she knew a starlet or two. When I called Sabie and told him my problem, he said, "I've got just the right girl for you. She's new in the school. She was raised in Holland and Germany, and she's got a great accent. You'll like her."

He sent me her composite. I wasn't thrilled with it but he talked me into at least trying her out. So, I booked her for a day the following week, and that's how I met Winnie Hart, the name Sabie had given Gertrude W. Behmenburg.

For the shoot, I got the use of the Imperial Suite of the Conrad Hilton Hotel. It was gorgeous—newly built atop the hotel. Floor-to-ceiling windows, grand piano, great furniture, and marble floors. In 1959, it went for $1,000 a day, really big bucks in those days.

Winnie Hart showed up on time, completely prepared. We all liked her immediately: Carl Snyder, the client, Edna Snyder, his wife/stylist and I. Winnie was tall and stunning and did speak with a charming German accent. It was hard to believe she was only 18. I think the fact that she had lived through World War II in Holland and Germany gave her a maturity that American girls her age didn't have.

The shoot began. A couple of times Winnie looked uncomfortable while I draped a sheet around her, but she said nothing. It wasn't until some time later that I found out Sabie had never told Winnie she was supposed to be a nude model. I could have killed him. His only instructions to her were, "George is a good photographer. Do what he tells you to do." In the end, the shoot was a success and I got the results I wanted without showing too much skin.

Winnie and I kept in touch after that and I used her for shoots with some of my other clients. She made a wonderful nurse on one shoot. But she wasn't doing well financially with her modeling career and she decided to take a job as secretary/designer for Carl, with his satin sheet business. He was expanding his line to include satin nightwear.

Winnie did well as a secretary but her passion was to be a fashion model. Her idol was Suzy Parker, the top model of that day. All Winnie talked about was modeling

Wilhelmina, Chicago, 1960

and Suzy Parker. And Carl, the former public relations man, was getting a little tired of hearing about Suzy Parker.

So one day he promised Winnie he would help promote her modeling career. "I'll take you around to fashion people and agencies and see if we can get you going on this career. George will take some high-fashion pictures and I'll put together a package to promote you."

I wasn't doing much fashion photography at the time. But we all loved Winnie. She was the kind of person you wanted to help, even if she wouldn't ask for it. We got a wardrobe together and I took a series of pictures of her on location, all around town. I must say, the results were terrific and Winnie was delighted with the photos. We had a lot of fun, and I realized how hard she had been working to be another Suzy Parker.

Carl kept his promise to promote her. The first thing he did was to change her name. Her real name, Gertrude W. Behmenburg, sure didn't work and neither did Winnie Hart. What was the "W." for? Wilhelmina. And that's how Winnie became Wilhelmina.

Carl took her to be registered at Patricia Stevens, the top agency in town at the time for fashion models. Stevens sent her to other photographers who did fashion. They took test shots and liked what they saw. Patricia Stevens put together her first real fashion composite. It couldn't have looked better. Wilhelmina was on her way.

Not only did she look great, but she was always on time, always prepared and never played the prima donna. If a shoot ran a little overtime, it was O.K. with her. She was a joy to work with. It wasn't long before Wilhelmina was the top model in Chicago. Carl and I were thrilled at her success. When Chicago's powerhouse agent Shirley Hamilton got hold of her, I don't think Wilhelmina had a day off from then on.

After conquering Chicago, the next logical move was New York. There, no surprise to us, Wilhelmina was also an immediate success. I saw her soon after she moved to New York and learned she was already working in Europe! She would trade her

Manhattan apartment with models from Paris and Milan when they were in town and she was in Europe. It worked out well.

One night we were having dinner in New York and she said, "I can't stay out late. I have an early shoot with Irving Penn." Irving Penn was one of the great photographers of the 20th century. I said, "Can you believe how far you've come, Winnie Hart?"

I didn't see her much after that. Occasionally I would see her mother who still lived in Chicago and get an update. She bought her parents an apartment building when the money started rolling in.

The last time I was with her was when her own agency, Wilhelmina Models, Inc., was in full swing and she was President Wilhelmina. She gave me a tour of the agency and a composite of one of her models, Jessica Lange, for my 12-year-old son Ben, who was in love with Jessica.

The last time I talked to Winnie (we still called her Winnie though the modeling community had dubbed her Willy), it was in 1978. She was writing a book called *"The New You"* and wanted me to identify some of the early pictures that she was using in the book. I was delighted when she sent me a copy which she had inscribed, "Dearest George. Thank you so much for all your help and friendship. Love, Wilhelmina."

In the front of the book, she thanked some of the great photographers (her words) with whom she had worked. I was pleased to be in the same company with Irving Penn, Victor Skrebneski and Bert Stern.

Two years later, in 1980, Winnie died of lung cancer at the age of 40. Suzy Parker died in 2003 at 69. What a shame Winnie could not have copied her idol in one last respect—a long life.

Burt Lancaster. I had admired actor Burt Lancaster ever since I had seen him in the movie *"The Killers."* When I got an assignment from INP to photograph him promoting the sale of Christmas Seals to help fight tuberculosis, I was thrilled. He was appearing at the Oriental Theatre in connection with his new film, *"Jim Thorpe: All-American,"* and made some time for the photos between appearances.

Burt Lancaster, 1951

INP had given me the poster to put up and envelopes showing prominent Christmas seals for him to hold. In the short time I was doing this, we had a chance to talk.

Between 1932 and 1939 he had toured vaudeville as an acrobat and from 1939 to 1942 had played in circuses with Nick Cravat in another act they called *"Lang and Cravat."* In fact, Nick was performing with him here at the Oriental. I didn't know but later learned Burt had also worked in Chicago as a salesman at Marshall Field's, as a fireman, and in a meatpacking plant. We had something in common.

As I told him what to do for the photos, I chuckled to myself. I was directing Burt Lancaster!

After the shoot, he invited me to watch his act from backstage. As he climbed to the top of a two-story high pole held by his partner and performed extremely difficult gymnastic positions at the top of it, I tried to understand why the hell a major movie star would do this. And then I remembered that he told me how much he loved doing his own movie stunts because he was a trained acrobat. That was the reason, plain and simple.

Jeff Chandler was a huge movie star in the '50s. When I met him in 1950, his latest role was Cochise, the famous Apache Indian chief in the movie *"Broken Arrow."* Chandler was making a personal appearance at the State & Lake Theatre where the film was being shown and I was shooting publicity pictures for 20th Century Fox. Chandler was very pleasant and low key. In spite of super stardom, he was definitely not a prima donna.

I made several pictures of him, and then two of his friends showed up. But first, a little background.

The year before, Philippe Halsman, the *Life* photographer, had shot a very sexy *Life* cover of Janet Leigh, a beautiful young actress with a rising career. I fell in love with Janet Leigh from that picture. I would have really liked to know her. So, who shows up backstage at the State & Lake Theatre? Jeff Chandler's good friends, Janet Leigh and Tony Curtis.

It was one of the few times I've been in awe. The famous couple was just returning from their honeymoon. Well, I took their picture with Chandler. Suffice it to say, Janet was beautiful and Curtis wasn't. Plus he was wearing a pungent kind of perfume, Lucky Tiger Hair Tonic, I think, that made his hair very shiny. I kept wondering how Janet Leigh could have married that guy when she could have had anyone, including me? It was a shock, but I got over it.

Chester Gould created his iconic comic strip character, Dick Tracy, in 1931. Gould died in 1985 after drawing that strip for 46 years but the *"Dick Tracy"* comic strip has survived under three subsequent cartoonists: Rick Fletcher until 1983; Dick Locher, the *Chicago Tribune* editorial cartoonist, until 2011; and is now going strong under artist Joe Staton with his co-author Mike Curtis.

In 1950, I was working for *Guns Magazine* when I went out with a writer, Bill Edwards, to Chester Gould's farm and studio in Woodstock, Illinois. Edwards was doing a story on Gould and the type of guns and gadgets that Dick Tracy used. I was shooting the photographs.

Gould couldn't have been more cooperative. He answered all questions and did whatever I wanted for the pictures. He also came up with good information we hadn't thought to ask. He showed us the first cartoons that were published of Dick Tracy. (I think the drawing improved over the years.) He also told us the original title was to be *"Plain Clothes Tracy"* but was changed at the last minute to *"Dick Tracy."*

Gould also showed us a miniature graveyard that he had set up in his back yard. In it were little tombstones for all the characters in his comic strip that were killed over the years.

At one point, Mrs. Gould came to the door to say hello. Chester told us that she hated guns and wouldn't come near one. She laughed. "It's true. I hate guns." I wonder if Chester Gould ever told her we were from *Guns Magazine?*

Most people in Chicago call the bridge over the Chicago River on State Street the "State Street Bridge." If they stopped to look at a bronze plaque on either side of the bridge they would see it's the Bataan-Corregidor Memorial Bridge which is meant to honor the 7,000 Americans who died at Bataan during World War II.

In the summer of 1949, after major rebuilding, the Bridge was dedicated by *General Douglas MacArthur.* What a day. Mayor Martin H. Kennelly, a Democrat, and every other politician who could be there was there. I didn't actually meet MacArthur except to say things like, "Look over here, General." Or, "Wave to this side." I spent the whole day and part of the night following MacArthur. Alfred Eisenstadt was there for *Life* magazine. I also followed him around because he seemed to know the best places to be.

I was working for Charlie Nickels on the news side of INP and for Don Alford on the commercial side of INP. Don had a client for whatever the General did. He rode in a red Lincoln convertible (Ford Motor Company). The General's parade went down State Street (State Street Council). The parade continued onto Michigan Avenue (Michigan Boulevard Association). The General ended up at the Conrad Hilton Hotel (Hilton Hotel Corporation). Whatever I shot, there was a client for the picture.

There were motorcycles on both sides of General MacArthur's car. I ran alongside poking my camera in between them to shoot pictures. At one point, my camera bag got hooked on one of the motorcycles. I ran for a block attached to the motorcycle before I could get loose. The motorcycle cop never stopped.

With his rumpled hat, wrinkled trench coat, and corncob pipe which was never lit, MacArthur looked to me like an actor playing a general. He certainly was a ham. He wound up the trip with a speech that night at Soldier Field. It was quite a day for Chicago.

One summer morning in 1948, Mike Shea called me up and said he had an assignment for Black Star, a new picture agency, to go to southern Illinois for a few days to photograph *Paul Douglas,* an economics professor at the University of Chicago. He was running for the U.S. Senate as a Democrat. Mike asked me to come along and help. Black Star would pay all the expenses. He also said the magic words: "It should be fun." The next day we were off to southern Illinois in Mike's 1947 Buick convertible, with the electric windows and the top down, to meet up with Paul Douglas.

The candidate was traveling through the small towns of Illinois in a Jeep station wagon with a big loudspeaker on the roof, like the Blues Brothers did in the movie. I think the candidate was glad to see us. He needed all the publicity he could get.

The best way to describe Paul Douglas is Lincolnesque. At 56, he was tall, wrinkled, and impressive but with a shock of white hair. Unlike Lincoln, he didn't tell jokes. He was very serious and always seemed to be deep in thought. His only companion was Ted, whose last name I don't remember. Ted was burly, probably in his 50s, who took care of everything and made all arrangements. A no-nonsense guy. Then I found out he was also a plain-clothes cop who carried a concealed gun.

We all got along well but it wasn't like covering a movie star or a big-time politician. No blue suit and tie, just sport shirt and slacks. Douglas could have been one of the farmers. He would park his Jeep in the town square of a small town and make a speech through the loudspeaker. He spoke mostly about the economics of farmers. He knew his facts—the price of corn, hogs, or anything else to do with the incomes of farmers—and how to make things better for them.

The crowds were sometimes small, 20 or 30 people, but they were always respectful. They understood what Douglas was saying, but more than one farmer commented, "Too bad he's on the wrong side." Southern Illinois was mostly Republican. One farmer told me he liked what Douglas was saying, but there was no way Douglas could beat (Senator C. Wayland) "Curly" Brooks, the Republican. After his speech, Douglas would go around the town square to the barber shop or beauty parlor and give a little talk to whomever was there.

One night he gave a speech in a small town hall to a fairly large crowd who seemed to be impressed with his facts. When he finished, the crowd applauded, and one man hollered, "Let's have a hoedown!"

The fiddles, banjoes and guitars came out and some great country music was played. This was one of Douglas' better nights. He seemed to enjoy the fun and looked right at home. I'm sure he was the only Ph.D. there.

Then we moved on to the next stop. Mike and I had fun walking around those small rural towns. Everyone we passed would say "Howdy." We city boys weren't used to that but, after a few hours, we caught on and would walk down the street saying "Howdy" to everyone. We really got a kick out of that.

One night, while checking out the local nightlife, of which there was little, we heard a man in a tavern say to his friend, "Those boys are from another county looking for our girls." True. It's good we never stayed in any town more than one night.

When we were traveling, I drove the Buick with the top down. Douglas opted to sit in the back seat instead of riding in the Jeep, his white hair blowing in the wind. One time I took a curve too fast and slid off and back onto the highway. Douglas didn't say a word but smiled when I told him I would slow down.

The trip was a success, but I didn't realize at the time what a hell of a guy Douglas really was. I remember asking Ted one day what happened to Douglas' crippled left arm. War wound. That was it. I found out later that at the age of 50 Douglas pulled strings in Washington so that during WWII he could enlist in the Marines as a private.

He fought and was wounded in the South Pacific battle of Okinawa. He received both the Purple Heart and the Bronze Star, and was discharged in 1946 as a lieutenant colonel. After five operations they still couldn't get his arm fixed. And I thought he was just another politician I was driving around.

I can't help but think of people like John Wayne, who, I'm sure, really believed he was a war hero when *he* was acting those parts in the movies. Wayne won every battle on film, but when it came to the real war he knew how to get a deferment.

Douglas upset Curly Brooks and won the election by more than 407,000 votes. One factor that helped: Brooks refused to debate Douglas, so Douglas debated an empty chair, arguing both his own side and Brooks' side. Douglas later wrote, "Brooks' replies, as I delivered them, never seemed to have the cogency and force of my attacks."

Paul Douglas served three terms in the Senate and is considered one of our greatest senators. I was so lucky to have met him. At the time I would have been more humble if I had known more about him. He was one of a kind.

Erik Hesselberg is a name that probably won't ring a bell with most readers, but he was a man I was dying to meet. He was the navigator on Kon-Tiki—the only licensed seaman on board—and a real-life genuine adventurer. The Kon-Tiki was a balsa wood raft that Thor Heyerdahl and five other men built in Peru in 1947, from 500 year-old plans.

Heyerdahl's idea was to sail the raft from Peru to Polynesia to prove that the Polynesians originally came from Peru. It was a fascinating trip, later made into a movie, and several books were written about it. The crew of six sailed 4,266 miles on the open sea and reached the islands in 100 days, thus proving Heyerdahl's theory.

So when my friend Bob Howe, a P.R. man, called me to take pictures of Hesselberg who was making a personal appearance at Carson Pirie Scott (his client), I jumped at the chance. Hesselberg had written a book about his adventure and was there to promote it.

The store had built a half-scale model of the original Kon-Tiki to put on display for the occasion. There was a large crowd to hear Hesselberg's talk and to buy his book. Unfortunately, the publisher had sent the Swedish edition. Still, the store took many orders for the English version to be sent later.

Afterward, I was lucky to have lunch with Howe and Hesselberg. I told Hesselberg I was planning a trip to Mexico and asked how they handled the film on their voyage. He said I shouldn't have a problem in Mexico. When I told him I was planning to look for Mayan ruins in the Yucatan, his ears picked up and he gave me a few pointers on preserving film. Our meeting was short but it's one I'll always remember.

John Amber knew more about guns than anyone I've ever known. He was the editor of *Gun Digest,* a publication put out by Klein's Sporting Goods Company, a large Chicago retail and mail order company. It was from Klein's that Lee Harvey Oswald ordered the rifle he used to kill President John F. Kennedy.

John Amber,
with Gatling gun,
1951

John Amber also wrote articles for *Guns Magazine*. I first met him while I was shooting a photograph for a *Guns* article. Amber mentioned he had trouble getting good pictures of many of his guns. I told him I was sure I could please him and I did. That started a friendship that lasted several years.

There are tricks to getting all the detail of engravings and serial numbers on black metal or gold and silver. My training at Liquid Carbonic Company came in handy. For the next few years I photographed hundreds of guns, all very special ones: long guns, handguns, antique guns, machine guns, and even the Gatling gun Amber kept in his office. The Gatling gun was the first mechanical, hand-cranked machine gun, and the forerunner of the modern machine gun. Its use was first demonstrated by the North during the American Civil War.

Most of the pictures were for Klein's, but I also did many feature stories with John for *Guns Magazine*. Amber was also a famous hunter. He told me he was trying to set up a tiger hunt in India. Would I like to come along and take pictures? Of course I would. I was excited about going, but it never happened, I think, because of Indian politics. It's just as well. The tiger is my favorite animal. I wouldn't want to see one shot.

Many times I had thousands of dollars worth of guns in my studio, most of them works of art. I never knew people spent so much money on gold inlays and engravings on a gun. John Amber's life was guns. At his farm outside Chicago, John's collection numbered hundreds of guns and he also owned the machinery to repair or modify any gun.

He treated guns like precious jewelry. One time at his farm I was photographing a long gun for the cover of *Gun Digest*. We were outdoors. He laid the gun on a colorful rock for a background. After I photographed it, he picked it up and accidentally scratched the barrel. The scratch was so small you could hardly see it. But Amber actually had a tantrum. I think if I had scratched the gun, he would have shot me. It was scary.

Other than that, we got along well. I had to admire his knowledge of guns, and I learned more than I needed to know about them. It was certainly an experience knowing John Amber.

When *Barry Goldwater* was running for president in 1964, he spent a lot of time in Chicago. A P.R. friend of mine who was involved in his campaign asked me if I wanted to shoot pictures for it. Why not? When Goldwater would come to town with his wife and Barry, Jr., to make speeches and raise money, I made photographs of the candidate on several occasions.

I liked the man personally but didn't care too much for some of the people around him. Especially the Young Republicans. They were arrogant, rich kids—not my favorite kind of guys. I shot most of their political functions and a lot of "grip-and-grins."

For the uninformed, a "grip-and-grin" is a photo taken when two people get together for a picture, shake hands, look into the camera, and smile. At one night's fund raiser, I think every Republican politician in Illinois was there to have a grip-and-grin with Goldwater. I set up a camera and a couple of lights and they all lined up.

*Presidential candidate
Barry Goldwater,
1964*

Joan took their names, gave them a number and collected the money. I think it was five dollars each. They came one at a time, shook hands, smiled, and I clicked. Next. Each one took a couple of seconds. That was the only money I saw. Later, after Goldwater lost, I sent a bill for the rest of the photography I did—photographs of him, of his speeches and political events. No answer. I called my P.R. friend to see what was going on. She said a lot of times they count you as a volunteer, and you could expect your rewards if the candidate won. But I hadn't volunteered.

I wrote several letters and made phone calls to the National Headquarters. They finally gave up and paid me. It was the last time I worked for politicians, but I still think, as far as I was concerned, Goldwater was a considerate and kind man.

Adlai Stevenson II (right) and Estes Kefauver (left) win Democratic presidential and vice-presidential nominations in Chicago, 1956

Adlai E. Stevenson II and Adlai E. Stevenson III. I didn't know Adlai E. Stevenson II, but I liked him. I liked the way he talked. I remember seeing him being interviewed in his home by Edward R. Murrow on Murrow's *"See It Now."* Murrow was looking at an old Indian blowpipe which shot poison darts. Stevenson commented that the pipe "was a remarkable piece of ordnance." Who else ever spoke like that?

I photographed Adlai Stevenson II with Estes Kefauver winning the nominations for president and vice president at the 1956 Democratic convention. I don't know why Stevenson didn't choose John F. Kennedy for vice-president, but he left it up to the convention and they chose Kefauver and his coonskin hat instead. What a mistake.

A news photographer once took a famous picture of Adlai E. Stevenson II with his legs crossed and which showed the sole of his shoe. The sole had a hole in it. I was sent by a magazine to photograph his son, Adlai E. Stevenson III, in his office during the tumultuous 1968 Democratic convention in Chicago.

Adlai Stevenson III, 1968

At the time, Adlai III was state treasurer of Illinois and also a very pleasant person. When I told him my editor wanted me to get a picture of him showing the sole of *his* shoe with no holes, he said, "That's silly." I said, "I agree, but I had to ask." Though I didn't shoot his sole I made some very nice pictures of him.

Adlai III lived on Dearborn Parkway, just south of Lincoln Park where the rebellious 1968 convention protesters were camping. A good friend of mine lived two doors from his house. She told me that her house was filled with tear gas the previous night when the police chased the demonstrators out of the park.

I asked Adlai whether he had gotten "gassed last night?" He frowned. "Yes. I wish the mayor would leave them alone." I enjoyed meeting Adlai III. I always felt he was too nice to stay in politics.

I first met **Charles H. "Chuck" Percy** when I photographed him for the cover of *Finance* magazine. He was still in his twenties and president of Bell & Howell. "What do you want me to do?" he asked. The pictures came out very well.

Charles H. "Chuck" Percy, 1963

I shot him again some years later before he ran for governor of Illinois. Percy liked the pictures. When he decided to run for governor he called and asked me if he could use one of the later ones for his campaign posters and billboards. Of course he could.

I did get a kick out of seeing one of my pictures on a huge billboard in downtown Chicago. Unfortunately, Percy lost that election, but he later ran for and won a seat in the U.S. Senate which he held for 18 years. He was one of the very small group of politicians I liked.

The humanitarian judge. There are all kinds of judges in Chicago. *Judge Hyman Feldman* was one of the best. I photographed him for a picture story. The judge's courtroom was on Monroe Street, one block south of West Madison Street, the heart of Chicago's infamous Skid Row.

(r) Judge Hyman Feldman and Walter Kelley (l), on Chicago's Skid Row, 1958

Skid Row was a terrible area, running for about a mile west to the Chicago Stadium. Flophouses, cheap taverns, sleazy nightclubs, drunks lying around, all kinds of vice everywhere.

Every morning, Judge Feldman and his referee, Walter Kelley, would hear the night's previous cases which were mostly drunk offenses. I was surprised to see how he handled most of them. Instead of just locking up the offenders he would try, whenever possible, to help them.

He had so many repeaters that he got to know many of them by name and problem. The judge would keep them in jail long enough for them to get sober. Then he assigned a social worker who would do her best to find work for them, or at least a place where they could be fed and housed before the next time they got hold of a bottle of what they called "Sneaky Pete."

Judge Feldman would sometimes walk down Skid Row to check conditions and see if he could make things better. The men were always happy to see him because they knew he was their friend. It was a never-ending job, but I think he made a difference. He was certainly sincere about helping them. Skid Row is gone now. I don't know where all those men went, but wherever it is I hope they found another friend like Judge Feldman. He was a good person.

The *Uncommon Women.* In 1978 my wife Joan Kufrin, a freelance writer, and I landed a contract to do a book about nine legendary American women in the arts. Joan would interview them about their work. I would photograph them. The women included prima ballerina Maria Tallchief, flutist Eugenia Zukerman, poet Gwendolyn Brooks, opera star Roberta Peters, novelist/critic Mary McCarthy, conductor Sarah Caldwell, actress Julie Harris, artist Alice Neel, and jazz composer and pianist, Mary Lou Williams.

It was a great book. Joan did wonderful in-depth interviews with these fantastic women, and I was very happy with the pictures I took. The following are a few memories of each woman from the picture-taking side of our project—my experiences that weren't in the book.

Prima ballerina *Maria Tallchief* has been totally dedicated to the ballet since the age of 12, when she began studying with Bronislava Nijinska, sister of famed dancer/choreographer Vaslav Nijinsky. First as a dancer with the Ballet Russe de Monte Carlo, and later as prima ballerina with George Balanchine's New York City Ballet,

Maria Tallchief, Chicago, 1980

The many faces of Maria Tallchief, Chicago, 1979

Maria created breathtaking new performances of Firebird, the Snow Queen, the Sugarplum Fairy, as well as dozens of other roles.

Of that time, she has said, "You cannot dance and leave it. It doesn't mean going home and forgetting about it. You live ballet. You sleep ballet. Your whole life is that and nothing else."

When I met her, Maria was married to Chicago millionaire Henry "Buzzy" Paschen, Jr. and could have taken life very easy. Instead, in 1980, at age 55, she had begun her own ballet company in Chicago and worked incredibly hard to make it a success.

Maria let me photograph her and her company wherever and whenever I wanted. She was a joy to shoot. One day I sat with her in her office and took a roll of close-up expressions. Thirty-six pictures. When I developed the film and made a contact sheet for editing, I couldn't find one picture I wanted to eliminate. What a passionate, beautiful face. For an exhibit I had, I enlarged the whole contact sheet. I had never done that before.

I photographed flutist, *Eugenia Zukerman,* in her Upper West Side apartment in New York, and later at a concert in Ohio where she was the guest soloist. She was the youngest of "our" women but still had plenty to talk about. At the time, she was married to violinist/conductor Pinchas Zukerman, and they often performed together. Their good friend, world-famous concert violinist, Itzhak Perlman and his family lived upstairs of the Zukermans.

Eugenia was very easy to photograph and gave me no problems. I think she was happy to be interviewed without her more famous husband.

After we left her apartment and went downstairs I remembered I had to make a phone call. I didn't want to go back upstairs and bother Eugenia, so I asked the doorman if there was a phone in the lobby. There was, a pay phone. We all looked for change. The best we could come up with was two dimes and five pennies. I needed a nickel.

While we were standing there, a station wagon pulled up and a man on crutches got out. It was Itzhak Perlman who had just returned from the country with his family and was stopping to drop them off before going into the garage. He was wearing very worn-looking blue jeans and a sports-shirt.

Eugenia Zukerman, New York City, 1980

He asked what the problem was. I said I need a nickel for five pennies. He dug in his pocket and came up with a nickel and took my five pennies. I don't think he thought I knew who he was. I thanked him and said he looked different than when I had seen him with the Chicago Symphony Orchestra. Big smile.

Gwendolyn Brooks. I'm not a great one for poetry, but I really liked Poet Laureate of Illinois, Gwendolyn Brooks. She was very low-key and didn't want her picture taken. When she realized she would be the only person in the book without a picture, she reluctantly said yes. Gradually, she loosened up. We had a mutual friend and that helped. By the time we finished the shoot, we were friends.

When the book came out, the *Chicago Tribune* wanted to excerpt the chapter on her in their *Sunday Magazine*. But all the pictures in the book are black and white, and the *Tribune* needed a color shot for the cover.

Gwendolyn Brooks, Chicago, 1982

This time there was no problem making a picture of Gwendolyn. "Come on over and shoot what you want," she said. I must say I made a great cover picture. She called me later to ask for some prints of it because, she said, it was her favorite picture. That made me happy.

Roberta Peters,
St. Louis,
1980

Roberta Peters, for 30 years the Metropolitan Opera coloratura soprano, is a perfect example of my favorite saying, "The harder you work, the luckier you get." I shot her at her home in Scarsdale, New York, and at a performance of *"The Merry Widow"* in St. Louis. I must have an honest face. Like most of our other women, she did whatever I asked. They were all happy with the results. I'm happy to say, Roberta Peters made my job easy. All she wanted to do was sing.

Mary McCarthy. What a woman. What unforgettable stories she told us: about her terrible childhood, about her brother Kevin McCarthy (the famous movie actor), running away from their abusive guardians *to* an orphanage; her second husband Edmund Wilson shutting her up in a room to make her start writing her first novel (he didn't lock the door); the only best selling book she had—*The Group*—sold 160,000 copies and she didn't like it very much at all.

Mary McCarthy and her then husband, James West, lived part-time in Paris and part-time in Maine. I photographed her in Maine. I would have preferred Paris, but I like Maine too. You get better lobster there. What impressed me most was the French maid they brought with them from Paris. She was a genuine French maid. She didn't speak English.

I made several pictures of Joan interviewing Mary in the living room of her beautiful 1805 Federalist house.

Then I asked her if I could get a shot with her at the typewriter in her den. (That was B.C., before computers.) She didn't like the idea. I thought maybe the den was messy, so I told her I didn't care if it was a mess, I just wanted to get some close-ups. "Well," she replied, "it's not a pigsty. Come on upstairs."

(l-r) Joan Kufrin and Mary McCarthy, Castine, Maine, 1980

Mary McCarthy, 1980

We entered this beautiful room with a fireplace, a window with a great view, and which looked as though it had been done by a decorator. I wouldn't be surprised if Washington had slept there.

I had her sit at her desk with the typewriter. We talked as I took the pictures. I don't remember what we talked about because, as I said before, when I'm concentrating on taking a picture it's difficult to listen.

I do remember telling her about the time my wife Joan and I were in a fancy Hollywood restaurant when Kevin McCarthy came in with a beautiful actress. Everyone around us, except Joan, was thrilled to see the movie star. She was excited to see Mary McCarthy's brother.

The pictures at her desk turned out to be the best ones. When we came downstairs Joan murmured to me, "You were up there a *long* time."

The highlight of our visit came after the interview and photos. Mary McCarthy invited us to have cocktails with her and Jim. I said I'd like a martini. She asked if I was a real martini drinker. Yes ma'am, for many years. She said, "Then I'll make you one," and she did. Chilled glass, lemon rubbed on the rim, really good gin and a pinch of vermouth, and stirred in the ice just long enough to cool but not dilute it. It was the best martini I've ever had. Later that evening, Mary called our hotel. She had made reservations for us at the best restaurant in town for lobster.

The first thing the conductor of the Opera Company of Boston, *Sarah Caldwell,* announced to me when she came into the room was, "You're not going to take

Sarah Caldwell, Boston,
1980

my picture." I had already started to unpack my camera. A brand new Hasselblad. For noncamera bugs, a Hasselblad is a very fine and expensive Swedish camera with German lenses. The astronauts took one to the moon. I didn't know that Sarah was a serious amateur photographer. That helped me. She said, "At least you have good equipment."

She seemed self-conscious about having her picture taken, but she had a very interesting face. She also tried to act like a tyrant, but after I got to know her I found her to be a pussycat. After a little prodding about the photos she finally gave in.

There was a picture window in the room with beautiful soft light coming in. I sat her facing the window. I didn't need any lights. Once she started talking with Joan, she forgot about me, and I got all the pictures I wanted. She was happy with them and later let me photograph her in Boston during an opera rehearsal. I met her mother there. She had seen the first pictures and said, "Those are the best pictures Sarah ever had." All's well that ends well.

I photographed actress *Julie Harris,* who has received five Tony Awards, three Emmy Awards, one Grammy and an Academy Award nomination, in her New York City apartment opposite the Plaza. To Julie, acting is a religion and the theater is the church. She's a brilliant actress and deadly serious about acting. I didn't dare make any jokes about the theater as I might have with another actor.

When she took a break from the interview I went out with her to walk her little dog. We were walking past Bonwit Teller when a very tall, well-dressed man stared at us, then said to Julie, "Are you who I think you are?"

She replied, "Who do you think I am?" "Julie Harris." She laughed and said yes, whereas he told her how much he admired her, was so grateful for her acting and mentioned several of her plays he had seen. He was obviously a real fan and she was very gracious.

A few weeks later I shot her in Washington at the Kennedy Center where she was rehearsing a new play, *"Mixed Couples,"* by James Prideaux, which also starred Rip Torn and Geraldine Page. I watched and photographed the rehearsal and then went to her dressing room to shoot a few more pictures. I told her I thought the play was terrific and was sure it would be a hit. (Like I'm a critic.) Then I told her

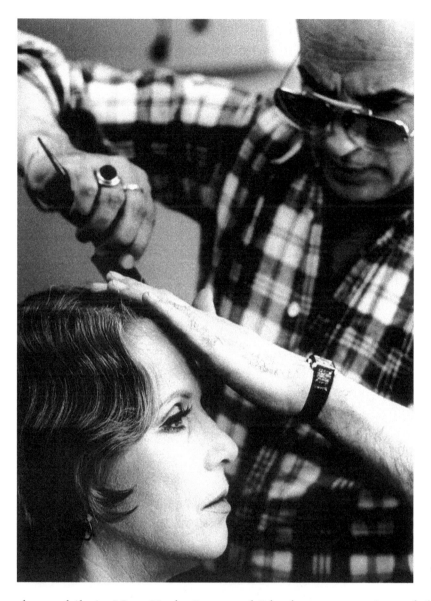

Julie Harris, New York City, 1980

that, while in New York, Joan and I had seen a preview of the new play George C. Scott was appearing in, *"Tricks of the Trade."* I said I thought that would be a sure hit too. She then informed me that it had closed opening night.

I wanted to fall through the floor. Next time I'll just shut up and take pictures. Julie was very generous and cooperative with me and, again, I was thrilled to know her. P.S. *Mixed Couples* opened on December 28, 1980 and closed January 3, 1981.

Alice Neel. I loved her. The minute we walked into her large studio and apartment on Upper Broadway, in New York City, I felt at home. It took me to my childhood and to my father's large studio. There is a certain wonderful smell to an artist's studio. I don't know all the ingredients it takes to make that smell, but it felt good to be there.

After Alice interviewed *us,* she wanted to know my nationality. When I told her my father was from Croatia, we had a long discussion about Croatia and Tito. After our interviews she had many wonderful stories to tell.

For the photos, she wore a bathrobe and slippers. She was more interested in her art than her looks, but I thought she looked fine. She had very few wrinkles for her age—then 81. Mostly, I photographed her in her studio where she paints. There were plenty of windows and shades to raise and lower so that I could adjust the

Alice Neel, New York City, 1980

daylight. It was a perfect photo studio. I didn't need any lights. In fact, most of the pictures in the book are made with natural light.

There isn't much more I can say about Alice from a picture standpoint. It was almost too easy. I got wonderful shots of her—including the photograph of her caressing the skull, which she suggested we do.

I was happy just listening to the interviews she did with Joan. All the pictures in the book are black and white, but for some reason I shot a roll of color of her. I'm glad I did. It really shows her and her work in the best light. There was only one Alice Neel and I was lucky to meet and photograph her. She died three years later.

Mary Lou Williams. I've placed her last here, but she is far from least. She was a true living legend. There isn't a jazz musician alive who doesn't owe Mary Lou. She was involved in all forms of jazz. Spiritual, ragtime, blues, swing, and BeBop. A jazz pianist who began playing when she was three years old, she performed with and arranged for just about every important jazz musician: Benny Goodman, Duke Ellington, Count Basie, the Dorsey brothers, Jimmie Lunceford, Charlie Parker, Dizzy Gillespie, Louis Armstrong, and others.

Mary Lou was the most challenging subject because she was ill and in the hospital in Durham, North Carolina, where she was artist-in-residence at Duke University. Her manager, friend, and confidant, Father Peter O'Brien, a Jesuit priest, had set up the interviews. I told him I didn't want to photograph her in a hospital bed. It wouldn't do her justice. He insisted that it was her wish. I said, "OK, but when she gets out of the hospital I'll come back and re-shoot her at home."

He agreed. Before we went to the hospital we stopped by her beautiful little house. On one wall was a colorful necktie in a frame autographed to her from "Pops." Louis Armstrong liked being called "Pops," "Satchmo," or "Louis" but hated being called "Louie."

On another wall was a photo of Mary Lou at a piano taken when she was in her prime by the famous photographer W. Eugene Smith. I was impressed and knew I could get better pictures of her right here at her home.

Still, at the hospital Mary Lou was alert, and Joan got one of the best interviews in the book, even though I couldn't help butting in. I'm a big jazz fan and had

Mary Lou Williams,
Durham,
North Carolina, 1980

known, or at least seen, many of the people she talked about. I did the best I could with the hospital pictures. They weren't bad. I wish I could have had more time to talk with her but I looked forward to shooting her again in her home.

A couple of weeks later, Father O'Brien called me, and we made a date. I had the plane ticket in my pocket when he called again to say she would not be leaving the hospital. I was very disappointed and very sad for her. Mary Lou died on May 21, 1981.

My part of *Uncommon Women* was now finished.

While writing this chapter I have often referred to *Uncommon Women* to check a name or date. I ended up reading the whole book again. It seems more relevant today than when it was published in 1981. It's long out of print, but you may find a copy on the Internet. It's a wonderful book. I hope Joan will have it reprinted.

My father, **Paul Kufrin,** was the least ordinary person I ever knew and I knew him all my life and most of his. In spite of the economic set-backs he endured during the Great Depression, he never stopped being an artist, never gave up on America.

He went from designing the great bronze doors for the Federal Reserve Bank on LaSalle Street in the '20s, and creating the relief decorative panels of the Assyrian Room at the Field Museum, to Franklin Roosevelt's W.P.A. (Works Progress Administration), creating a pair of fierce polished granite eagles to guard the U.S. Post Office on Broadway Avenue in Chicago.

During the war he worked as a mechanical draftsman for Borg-Warner doing defense drawings. He taught anatomy and sculpture to women's art classes. Became president of the Palette & Chisel Academy and was a fervent and vocal member of the Sanity in Art movement. He denounced Tito, the dictator of Yugoslavia (which included his homeland, Croatia) constantly and openly.

After losing his American Studio in the Depression, he never had a studio again. When he was commissioned to do a bust of George Cardinal Mundelein, he created the clay model in our kitchen.

In 1946, he became lead sculptor in sculpting the clay model of the new Tucker automobile, a futuristic car to be built in Chicago. The Tucker concentrated on safety, a rear engine, a pop-out windshield in case of a collision, three headlights (the middle one turned when the car did), disc brakes and other futuristic features. Only 50 Tuckers were ever sold, but my father remained enthusiastic about it, even as the company failed.

His last commission was his largest. At 70, he created huge cement panels depicting the history of cement for the Portland Cement Association Research Center. The panels still welcome visitors at the company's headquarters in Skokie, IL.

A highlight of his life came in 1965, when Herman Kogan, founding editor of the *Chicago Daily News Panorama* magazine, featured my father's work in an article entitled, "A Life's Work in Stone," written by Joan Kufrin. She and my father traveled all over Chicago, visiting his work, the sculpture that time had demolished and the work that was still standing. It was a life-affirming moment for him.

I remember how he loved founding father Thomas Paine and can still hear him repeating Paine's quote: "The world is my country; all mankind is my brother; and to do good is my religion."

He died in 1973 and I still miss him.

Paul Kufrin, with his work at the Portland Cement Association Research Center, Skokie, Illinois, 1965

CHAPTER ELEVEN

Old Town

For six months during the 1950s, I roomed with one of the kindest, funniest and sweetest persons I've ever known. Bobby Kotalik. He was also a smartass and a hugely talented photographer with a 47-year career with the *Chicago Sun-Times,* much of that time as chief photographer. In those early days, he looked a little like a tall Spike Jones, the zany bandleader who spoke in weird sound effects. (Yes, I photographed Spike once.)

Everyone who knew Bobby loved him. And he was always ready to do you a favor. You needed a place to stay for a night or two? You could count on Bobby. In fact, I never knew who would be coming home with him. Often it was Carmen Reporto. "Casanova Carmie" was one of the *Sun-Times'* top photographers, a friend to politicians and a shrewd businessman who later made a fortune in real estate.

There was a lot of traffic in that apartment. For awhile, it was fun living there. However, after six months, I got myself organized and decided I needed more privacy. So I rented an apartment in Chicago's Old Town. There was a saying that the boundaries of Old Town were whatever was within the sound of St. Michael's church bell. But in reality, Old Town was (and still is) an area west of Lincoln

Johnny Weissmuller, Chicago, 1965

Park, from Clark Street west to Orleans, and from Armitage Avenue on the north to Division Street on the south.

In the mid-'50s, many artists, writers, designers and other creative and talented people lived in Old Town. Its shabbiest section was Wells Street, south of North Avenue to Division Street, lined with many empty storefronts and eclectic businesses.

It was here that I found my apartment. A four-rooms-plus-bath apartment on the second floor of one of those storefronts wasn't much, but it was all mine.

My Wells Street neighbors included a parking garage, a used bookstore, a woodworking factory, a Standard Oil gas station directly across from my apartment, a Mexican diner and a store that sold rabbits and other live produce. On the corner of Wells and Division, Chicago's oldest wine merchants, the House of Glunz, founded in 1888, was—and still is—doing business.

One block east of me, on Clark Street at Goethe, was the tiny SRO Lounge, where Ramsey Lewis and his Trio played a six-night-a-week gig. I patronized SRO (and also a Chinese laundry on Clark Street) frequently.

One block west, the Dr. Scholl's factory turned out 400 different foot care products, and over on Sedgwick and Division, the Oscar Mayer factory was squeezing out 200 varieties of sausages, lunchmeats, and smoked and canned meat products.

I loved living on Wells Street. But within a year, urban renewal had begun to rear its head. The idea behind urban renewal was to protect a stable neighborhood from further encroachment of "blight," i.e. run-down, low-rent structures a.k.a. slums, that adjoined it. It was the catalyst that would change Old Town forever.

In this case, the City of Chicago exercised its eminent domain power and cleared (demolished) all the structures between Division Street and North Avenue along Clark Street and La Salle to buffer or protect the adjoining Gold Coast from advancing "blight."

No matter that many of the demolished structures were once-beautiful old row houses (that had been turned into rooming houses) still had priceless and historic interiors of hardwood, marble and stained glass. The city then opened the cleared area to bids for development.

A bid of $6,411,000 from Arthur Rubloff and his investor group won the right to build 3,166 high rise rental units on the cleared land (that would ultimately be known as Sandburg Village, after the poet Carl Sandburg).

One very savvy entrepreneur and friend of mine, *John Moody* who, to me, looked just like the comic strip character, *"L'il Abner,"* made the most of the opportunity to salvage beauty from the wrecker's ball. John had previously been a bartender at the Old Town Ale House on North Avenue. When he decided to open his own Moody's Pub, he rented a Wells Street storefront and furnished it with doors and woodwork from those once-beautiful row houses on North Clark Street.

For tables in his tavern, he used giant wooden spools which Commonwealth Edison wound wire cable on. And his chairs were school chairs from the Catholic Charities store.

Moody's Pub was unique. It caught on immediately and became a major watering hole for the neighborhood. Later, decorators would try to duplicate Moody's "look." They never succeeded.

Both the Ale House and Moody's thrived for several years. I spent time at the Ale House, but I was a regular at Moody's. I liked the way John did business. He kept a little account book, like grocers did during the Great Depression. Your credit was good if he knew you. He would remind you when your account page was full and it was time to pay up.

Both taverns encouraged local artists to hang and sell their paintings and you could pick up some real bargains.

I often thought a description of how I was living then would make a funny story. Many days when I had to photograph a VIP (board chairman, bank president), I would get up in the morning, put on my Brooks Bros. suit, my Burberry trench coat, and get into my red MG TD convertible[1] which had a hard top for cold weather.

After driving downtown to the job, I would often have lunch afterward, courtesy of the client, in an executive dining room, or at the Union League Club, or the

---

[1] That MG was the most fun two-passenger car I ever owned. It never carried more than five people. I kept it for about a year but finally had to face reality. In the winter I froze to death and there was no decent luggage space for my equipment. I sold it for $1,000, exactly what I paid for it, and bought a Hillman Husky, a small English station wagon that looked like a box on wheels. The Hillman came with a "starting handle," which Americans call a crank. If the battery died (rarely), I could easily start the four-cylinder, four-speed engine with the crank.

University Club. Then I'd go back to the studio, change my clothes, and work in the darkroom for a few hours. I'd end the day in my khakis, sweatshirt and sneakers at Moody's Pub, roasting a hotdog in his fireplace and drinking with friends. I felt like a chameleon, but I made many lifelong friends at Moody's.

Bill Koen, a terrifically talented artist and devil-may-care free spirit, became one of my best friends. With his dog Aristophanes, he lived and painted in a one-room studio complete with a loft and skylight, in a building situated between a hardware store and an undertaker.

Phil Rowe, a metal sculptor virtuoso with an acetylene torch, was another. *Roger Burgos,* first a resident at Cook County Hospital, later a radiologist on staff there, was an unforgettable man and close friend.

Federico Camacho, a stocky, kind-hearted man who looked more Mayan than Spanish, emigrated from Salina Cruz (Oaxaca), Mexico in 1946. He opened a Mexican restaurant, Café Azteca, in an old three-flat on North Avenue near Wells in 1957.

Federico was another genius who could make something out of nothing. With little money, he transformed the first floor of the storefront into a charming restaurant and the back yard/trash heap at the rear of the building into a beautiful patio.

"Federico Camacho, your host" (it said on the menu and match covers) also played the guitar and the marimba, and he sang like a bird. Café Azteca was one of three sit-down Mexican restaurants in Chicago at the time, and one of the first to cater to gringos. Federico insisted that his waiters learn some English. He later told me those same waiters didn't think he would make it because the restaurant wasn't located in a Mexican neighborhood.

The truth is that Café Azteca wasn't doing very well until the night Wil Leonard, an Old Town resident who was also a columnist for the *Chicago Tribune,* came in. He tried the chicken soup and loved it, declaring it the best soup he had ever eaten. He also raved about it in his column the next day and the Azteca was on its way. It didn't hurt that Federico also made the best Mexican food of any I've ever had and I've had a lot.

Federico Camacho, 1963

I met Federico for the first time when Café Azteca was brand new, and we became friends for life. I often took publicity pictures for the restaurant and also First Communion pictures of his daughters. He paid me in tacos.

He always called me Jorge (hor-hay). I had learned a little Spanish in the Merchant Marines and was eager to learn more. I practiced my Spanish with the waiters and they practiced their English with me. We had a lot of laughs correcting each other. Federico spoke excellent English and also helped me with Spanish. I loved to go to the Azteca.

One day Federico said he was planning a Christmas Posada, and he wanted me to be in it. "What's a Posada?" I asked.

He explained. "We recreate Joseph and Mary's journey looking for a place to stay in Bethlehem. We have Joseph, Mary riding a donkey, the Three Wise Men, and many pilgrims walking through the neighborhood. We stop at designated homes where we sing Mexican Christmas carols. The people in the homes come out and give us hot drinks and then send us on to the next house. Everyone is in costume. We have a lot of fun."

Jokingly, I said, "Sure, but I want to be St. Joseph." To my surprise, Federico said OK. On the day of the Posada there was a terrific snowstorm. That night everyone showed up at the Azteca where we dressed up in the costumes Federico had rented, over layers of sweaters. Federico had also rented a donkey. The streets were heavy with snow, and it was freezing cold.

With several guitars accompanying us, we began the march along North Avenue to our first stop: Albert Cardinal Meyer's residence, a beautiful Victorian mansion on North State Parkway. We made a colorful procession with me at the head, leading the donkey with Mary aboard.

Federico's Posada, with GK as St. Joseph, circa 1961

The Posada was something new for Old Town. We had a police escort and I heard one cop say, "I don't know what the hell it is. I was just told to give them an escort." All the newspapers showed up and photographed us, with St. Joseph prominent in the foreground.

Cardinal Meyer wasn't at home that night but several nuns and priests came out from the mansion to sing carols with us. Then we moved on through the neighborhood, stopping along the way at several homes where we were expected.

At each stop people welcomed us with hot coffee, cider, and booze to pour into the cider. Naturally, St. Joseph was the first one to be served. By the time we got to our last stop, the nuns' residence at St. Michael's Church, I didn't need any sweaters. I was very warm.

The nuns came out and sang carols with us, then invited us into the church hall for coffee and snacks. The Mother Superior came up to me and said, "So you're St. Joseph." With Federico looking on, I repeated to her several times that, no, I was George. I wasn't *really* St. Joseph. I was just playing the part of St. Joseph.

Federico was so embarrassed and mad at me he told me I would never be in his Posada again. I felt terrible because the Posada quickly became a very large and popular annual Christmas event in Old Town. The good news is Federico forgave me and a couple of years later let me be a Wise Man.

Not only was Café Azteca a big success, but so was Federico. Over the years, he bought up a lot of real estate around North Avenue and Wells Street. When the original restaurant was torn down to make room for a supermarket on land he owned, he moved across the street and built a larger Café Azteca and patio, also on land he owned. Success could not have happened to a nicer guy.

Even as I was helping him plant peach and pear trees in the new patio, I sadly informed him they would never grow in the shade cast by two buildings on either side. I'm here to say those trees grew so tall he had to keep cutting them back. Federico could make anything grow. Even hundreds of colorful flowers grew everywhere in that shady patio.

For those who have never heard Mexican mariachi music, I am sorry. Mariachis are a group of strolling musicians, often dressed in silver-studded charro outfits and wide-brimmed hats. They play violins, guitars, trumpets, basses, and maybe a *viheula* (a five-string guitar) as they sing wonderful songs about love, death, betrayal, politics, the passing of time, friendship. To me, it is the best music in the world. I love mariachis.

Many times, when people celebrated a special occasion at the Café Azteca, Federico would hire a mariachi band for the festivities. But he would be sure to call me ahead of time so that I could have dinner at the restaurant that night and hear them. One night, my wife and I went to the Azteca for dinner and I saw mariachis waiting. "Why didn't you call me?" I asked Federico. "I might have missed them." He laughed. Joan had hired them as a surprise for me.

I still miss Federico Camacho. We were close friends until he died in 1989.

This was a great time for all the free spirits living on and around Wells Street. Then, around 1962, something happened. Maybe it was the A-bomb testing that provoked it, but all of a sudden matrimony broke out.

Everyone started getting married. My friend, Bill Koen with the German Shepherd, Aristophanes, married *Mary Wartman,* with her Saint Bernard, Heidi. Phil Rowe married *Germaine Garbisch. Carol Reese* married *Wayne Warga.* My friend Ernie married *Barbara Segal* who would open her new Wells Street bookstore, "Barbara's Bookstore," in 1963. *Fredi Mohr,* the artist, married candy and gum magnate *Marshall Leaf.* Eventually, even *Bobby Kotalik* on Dearborn Street would marry his *Pearl.* The most creative twosome was *Leroy* and *Sally.* Leroy had vowed never to get married so Sally had her last name legally changed to his last name. It made her life simpler.

And I married *Joan Yarbrough,* the writer.

Joan Kufrin, 1962

Even married, it was still fun living in Old Town, though different. Joan and I moved into the Marshall Field apartments on Sedgwick Avenue in Old Town, but I soon started to look for more space where we could live and work. I didn't have much luck until I ran into my friend Otto, a regular at Moody's.

He told me he was working in a new little store that just opened. It was in an old building on Wells Street, built right after the Chicago Fire in 1871. He said the top two floors were for rent. It was worth a look.

I went to the new little store, the "Crate & Barrel," and met *Gordon Segal,* the owner. He was selling dishes and glassware from around the world, using the crates and barrels they had been shipped in as display cases. Hence the name. Gordon thought it would be a good idea to have a photographer upstairs. He gave me the name of his landlord.

I was eager to see the place but when I got inside, what a mess. Throughout the years the building had been used as an elevator factory and also as a chicken-plucking factory. It was shabby and filthy.

The front of the two floors took up about 20 percent of the building. The back part had originally been a huge German meeting hall, known in the 1870s as Centerfelder Hall. It was about 100 feet long, 30 feet wide, with a 25-foot ceiling. At some point, someone had put in a floor which cut the big room in half. This meant that now there were two 100-foot long rooms, each with a ceiling about 12 feet high.

It had more than enough square feet, but I didn't know what to do with it. I went back several times and just sat and stared at it. I finally figured out what might work.

It would be a big, expensive project, but if I could get cheap rent it would be worth it. I would tear out the ugly floor that was added years before and bring the room back to its original size, but I would also leave part of it for a large balcony. We would live upstairs and have a darkroom and studio below. It could be beautiful.

I called our friend Fredi, the artist who introduced Joan and me, to come over and look at what I planned. She was one of the few people who said I wasn't crazy. She drew a beautiful rendering of how the place would look when finished. And on

Wells Street studio (before), 1964

The "Buffalo" at work, 1964

paper, it really did look fantastic. I took the rendering to **Don Plantico,** the owner of the building who also owned a small elevator company nearby.

Don was impressed. I said, "Let me do this and I'll give you two hundred dollars a month rent." He smiled and replied, "A hundred and fifty." Now that's my kind of landlord. Don also volunteered to help with some of the demolition. We signed a lease.

Now what do I do? I'm not a contractor. The first thing to do was tear out the old floor that had been added. Don sent over a big burly guy he called The Buffalo. I never did know his real name. The Buffalo did most of the tearing out of the floor.

I'll never forget the night he tore up enough of the floor so that we could see just how high the ceiling was going to be. It was so high it was scary. The ceiling even had a dome! I kept wondering, "What the hell do I do now?"

The work went slowly. There was insulation in the ceiling that was flying all over the place. But once the added floor was out, and all the insulation cleaned up, things started to look hopeful.

Most of our friends still thought I was crazy. But I remember the day my father came by to see what I had been up to. He walked into this huge dirty, dusty mess and proclaimed, "Now *this* is a studio." He loved it and could see what it would be.

This was a tight budget project. We had to put in a bathroom and kitchen. The kitchen and dining room would be on the balcony. The bedroom and bathroom were in the original part of the building.

I read in the paper that WGN was moving their television studio and selling the contents of all their TV sets. They had a large kitchen set for their cooking shows that included a large sink and every kind of lighted cabinet you'd ever want or need.

We bought the whole set for fifty bucks. Did we have a kitchen! The only drawback was we had to repaint over the flat gray paint that WGN had used to take the gloss off the shiny metal cabinets for its black and white TV cameras.

We "harvested" dozens of hardwood 2x12s from the old ceiling and were able to use them all in the renovation. Some became a stairway to the balcony. Sam, whom Don had located for us, was a carpenter employed by Cook County. His job: building wooden coffins for bodies that were sent to Potters Field. Sam built our stairway in one evening out of several of the 2x12s.

Other boards I used to build solid pillars to brace the balcony from underneath. Still others went into an 80" long bar, a solid and handsome natural division between our kitchen and dining area.

The whole renovation project took almost a year, but when it was finished it came out better than I ever imagined. We had great living quarters, a great darkroom and a studio. The *Chicago Herald American* did a full-page feature story on it.

Downstairs, Gordon gave me a couple of crates and barrels that I used for props in my studio. He was doing really well. He told me he wanted his store to be like George Jensen's. I must say he had (and has) wonderful merchandise. We still have a couple of pots we bought then.

Gordon and his wife Carol, and Joan and I celebrated their first successful year with drinks in the storeroom basement. Everyone was happy.

Wells Street studio (after), 1965

The next summer his business was so good that he put in a giant air conditioner. That was a big problem—for me. When he turned it on there was no water pressure upstairs. It was bad enough that we couldn't take showers then, but I couldn't develop my film or make prints.

I would have to work past midnight when the damn thing was off. Then it would start up again early in the morning in the middle of our showers. Gordon and I had a big hassle over that until our landlord finally put in a pump.

A couple of years later Gordon built a new store two doors down the street, and I thought he had found a permanent home. Who could guess it was the start of a national chain? I give him a lot of credit. He knew what he was doing. When the Crate & Barrel left, Don rented the downstairs store to his girlfriend, who opened a candy store. She named it "The Candy Store."

When I was a kid, I loved growing up in a neighborhood where I knew everyone and couldn't walk down the street without meeting someone I knew. Wells Street was like that when we lived there. It was a genuine close-knit neighborhood, and we loved it. With few exceptions, our neighbors were not boring people.

I think of *Bruno Gasiorowski* who built a 30' sailboat, based on the design of an ancient Polynesian outrigger canoe. He built it in his long, narrow, third-floor Old Town apartment. Each end of the boat was identical except for the stunning figureheads he hand-carved for each bowsprit. (One was a man, the other a woman.)

The boat flew one large triangular lateen sail, the same kind of sail used by medieval navigators, and which allowed him to sail easily on either side of the wind.

The only way Bruno could get the boat out of his apartment was to have a crane lift it out the window. Local TV stations covered the event and once the boat was launched I made photographs of the historic vessel on Lake Michigan.

Then there was *Germaine Rowe,* our friend and neighbor down the block. Germaine called one afternoon to ask if she could come by and boil some potatoes on our stove. The gas company had shut hers off. She arrived with the potatoes in a pot, and even brought her own water. While the potatoes boiled, we all had martinis.

Left to right; Bruno Gasiorowski on bowsprit of his hand-built sailboat; The 30' vessel under sail on Lake Michigan, circa 1964

Margaret Garbisch was Germaine Rowe's sister and was studying to be a concert pianist. When Germaine married Phil Rowe, Margaret had to get a smaller apartment, but couldn't find one that would hold her grand piano so she made a deal with us. If we would pay to move the piano to our place which had plenty of space, she would pay to move it out when she could afford a larger place. In the meantime would we let her come over and practice? *Let* her?

She was a wonderful pianist and every Saturday morning played a free Bach or Beethoven concert for us. Besides enjoying Margaret's playing, we loved the way the piano enhanced the studio.

About six months later, Duke, the brother of ***Nancy Link,*** another friend from the neighborhood who owned the classy, upscale women's wear shop on Wells Street, "Horse of a Different Color," visited Nancy from California.

When Duke met Margaret, lightning struck. They fell instantly in love and in ten days were married and off to California. What to do with the beautiful grand piano? Margaret said, "I can't take it with me. Give me a hundred bucks and it's yours." We paid her in two installments. And kept it for 45 years.

The giant snowstorm of 1967 which dumped 36.5" of snow on us, crippled Chicago. Wells Street was completely shut down for several days with buses and cars stuck in the middle of the street with snow up to their roofs.

It was wonderful. It felt like having our own private small town. We had a few parties and we all helped each other shoveling snow and sharing food and drink. I told Joan that no snowplow was going to clear this street. It would need a D-8 Caterpillar tractor.

Sure enough, one morning we heard the loud roar of the D-8 pulling out buses and cars and removing snow. Our holiday was over.

Not long after this, Joan got an assignment to do a piece with pictures on *Johnny Weissmuller* who had lived in Old Town when he was growing up. What a thrill to meet the five-time Olympic Gold winner and the original Tarzan, whom Johnny played in nearly twenty Tarzan movies. We met him at the "Fireside Inn," a restaurant across the street from my studio. What a sweet, humble guy who had one powerful handshake.

Johnny told us about his childhood in the area. He would swim in Lake Michigan just a few blocks from Lincoln Park, which, he recalled, was once a cemetery. Across the street from where we were standing, Johnny pointed out there was once a building called a natatorium. It had a small pool where he often swam, but most of his swimming and Olympic training was done at the YMCA on North Avenue and Ogden.

Johnny was an adventurous, mischievous kid. He told of the times he and his friends would crawl up under the elevated train tracks, pop their heads up between the ties and scare the motorman to death, then duck down before the train hit them. Can you see a kid doing that today?

We then took a drive around Old Town. Johnny knew every street. I took several pictures of him on Wells Street, in front of St. Michael's church which he had attended as a child and in front of a small grocery store on Mohawk Street which had once been his father's tavern.

He stood looking at it for a long moment. He told us his father belonged to a German yodeling society, and that's where he got his famous Tarzan yell. That yell came in handy in 1967. Johnny was playing golf in Cuba during the Revolution, when he and his friends were surrounded by Fidel's soldiers, bent on kidnapping or worse. Thinking fast, Johnny erupted into his famous Tarzan yell. The soldiers recognized it—and Johnny—and escorted them to a safe area.

He told other stories about growing up in Old Town and said one of the best experiences of his life was swimming out and saving a kid from drowning off North Avenue beach. He also remembered his mother telling him not to drown when he went off to the Olympics![2]

It was obvious that he was feeling very nostalgic visiting his old neighborhood. Why have I been so lucky to meet so many great people? Johnny Weissmuller was one of my favorites.

Gradually Old Town began to change. At the time, it seemed for the better. I was shooting a lot of fashion ads, and the models no longer were afraid to come to my studio at night. I look at most of the fashion pictures I took 40 years ago and it's satisfying to see they hold up well today.

Besides the Café Azteca, a number of other good restaurants were opening—"The Beef & Bourbon," "That Steak Joint," the "Fireside Inn," and even the "Belgian Waffle Shop."

The Old Town Art Fair, the oldest art fair in the country, was held on the north side of North Avenue in Old Town. It brought more and more people every year, and many folks drifted south of North Avenue to check out the "new" and quaint Old Town. People liked it in increasing numbers. In fact, after a couple more years the crowds of tourists were so thick that on weekends we could hardly get out our front door.

Second City moved down from Lincoln Avenue to new, larger quarters on Wells Street, just off North Avenue. That brought in even more people. In 1957, my

---

[2] Besides five Olympic Gold medals, Weissmuller held 67 world and 52 national swimming titles.

friend **Win Stracke,** from *"Studs Place,"* had started his Old Town School of Folk Music in the old Immigrant State Bank Building on North Avenue just west of Wells Street. It was a growing success and that, too, brought more people to the neighborhood. North Avenue and Wells Street were beginning to look like State and Madison Streets.

Then came a sleazy period. Motorcycle gangs and drug users began hanging out at all hours of the morning in some of the new, less respectable joints that opened. Many tourists who came down to Wells Street thought it was a place where you could raise hell to the wee hours of the morning—and then go home. For those of us who lived there it became a nightmare.

Mary and Bill Koen leave Chicago for Maine, 1966

Our friends started to leave Old Town. Bill and Mary moved to Maine. We were sad to see them leave, but they did it with flair. One early Sunday morning they stopped by to say goodbye, their Volkswagen Bug filled to the roof with all their worldly possessions: including Aris, the German Shepherd and Heidi, the Saint Bernard. Talk about a full car.

We visited them in Maine several times where Bill was teaching art. We ate a lot of great lobster dinners together and hoped for many more. It was not to be. Bill died about ten years later of cancer. He was 47, much too young. Their son Seth, is our godson.

Five years ago, we made another nostalgic trip to Maine for Seth's marriage to Shelby and to visit Mary and her adventurer husband, Sandy Allen, who recently climbed Mt. Everest.

Leroy and Sally moved to Indiana. Phil Rowe and Germaine divorced and she moved to Oregon. Roger finished his residency and became a well-to-do doctor. He was one of the smartest and most literate persons I've ever known. Several years later, after a bitter divorce, he became a much less wealthy doctor. I felt his pain.

Wayne and Carol Warga moved to New York where Wayne became entertainment editor for *Life* magazine. They later moved to Los Angeles where Wayne had a similar job for the *Los Angeles Times*. Wayne was very helpful to me when I was there shooting fashion pictures on location. One year, he arranged for me to use the whole back lot at Universal Studios for the shoot. We, too, remained lifelong friends.

Fredi and Marshall moved to Dearborn Parkway, near Wells Street, but much quieter. The final departure was John Moody closing his pub and moving it a mile away to a quieter spot. His rent had been raised too, another incentive to leave, for John was never a big spender. He didn't need or want the tourist trade. Today he owns Moody's II restaurant and pub on the far north side of Chicago, far away from Old Town. And the last time I saw him, he still looked like Li'l Abner.

We left Old Town and bought a big 100-year-old Victorian house on Logan Boulevard for our growing family but I kept the studio on Wells Street. On Logan Blvd. we could sleep at night. I didn't even go down to Wells Street on weekends unless I had to. This worked out for several years, but it was lonely in that huge studio. Joan stayed home and did her writing and mothering to our two kids, Ben and Eve, and sometimes to my two kids, Paul and George.

One day I ran into Don, my landlord, and he looked terrible. He told me he wasn't feeling well. Later, I learned he had cancer. Two days after I saw him he went into the basement of the studio on Wells Street and shot himself. I really felt bad. I knew Don wasn't the type to lie in a hospital with tubes in him, but it was still a shock.

A couple of days later, Don's brother who lived out of town sent me a letter telling me to send him the rent. I knew then there were going to be hassles about who owned the property because Don's girlfriend thought she did.

Since I was doing more and more corporate and advertising work, mostly on location, I didn't need all that studio space. It was time to move on. The early years on Wells Street were some of the happiest years of my life, but that era was long gone. I rented smaller space downtown.

And other things had changed. I was no longer working with plain P.R. people. Now it was layers of public relations executives, account executives, and vice-presidents of this and that. There were exceptions, but most everything was becoming more complicated. I adapted and did well, but how I worked was definitely different.

These days, Joan and I go down to Wells Street occasionally for dinner. The honky-tonk has disappeared. Now it's big-bucks restaurants and high-priced condos. We have mixed feelings every time we go. We had so many good times there but it's sad to see how the places that once belonged to us have changed. Now we know how Johnny Weissmuller felt when he visited *his* Old Town neighborhood.

After the Old Town years—with its excitements and ambitions and achievements—life with our growing children would bring new and even more wonderful experiences for Joan and me. But that's an entirely different book.

This one is the story of their father before they really knew me. And I'll finish it here. By now, I hope you—and they—understand why I call myself "Lucky George."

Index

Shriner, Herb, 106
Sianis, Billy Goat, 25-26;
    role in hex on Cubs, 26
Snead, Sam, 121
Snyder, Carl, 79, 84, 86, 102, 107, 141,
    167-170
Soward, Curley, oiler, 49, 64-65
Speed Graphic camera
    assures entrance to Republican/
        Democratic conventions, 4;
    big break in fire photo, 17;
    role at the Billy Goat Inn, 26;
    usefulness in the Army, 139
Split, Croatia, (then Yugoslavia), 60
Staton, Joe, 173
Stauber, Rudy, 15, 16
Stevenson, Adlai II, 183
Stevenson, Adlai III, 183-184
Stock market crash of 1929, 8
Stowaways, 36, 56-57
Stracke, Win, 222
Swanson, Gloria, 3

Tallchief, Maria, 187-189
Terkel, Studs, 92-93
Thomas, Capt. Lewis E., 50
Thomas, Danny, 4, 87
Tormé, Mel, 88-89, 162
Townsend, Freddie, 76
Treacher, Arthur, 96
Truman, President Harry S., 137
Tsing Tao, China, 65-67
Tucker automobile, 201
Tucker, Sophie, 161
Twenty-second Ward, 9
Twenty-sixth Police District Court, 186

U.S. Marines and cat eyes, 35
U.S. Maritime Service Training Center, 29
U.S. National Atomic Reactor Testing
    Station, 152
U.S. Steel Corp., 146
Uncommon Women, 187
Union Planters National Bank, 125
Union Stock Yards, Chicago, 61

Vejvoda, Mae (Mary)
    emigration from Bohemia, 9;
    marriage to Paul Kufrin, 3
Venice, Italy, 57-59
Victorio, A.B., 49
Victory ship vs. Liberty ship, 38
von Braun, Wernher, 125

Waco, Texas, tornado, 140
Wallace, Mike, 92, 161
Walton Walk, 163
War brides, 42-43
War in Europe over, May 8, 1945, 31
Ward, Tom, 146
Warga, Carol Reese, 212, 223
Warga, Wayne, 212, 223
Wartman, Mary, 212, 222
Weissmuller, Johnny, 220-221, 224
Wells Street studio, 213-215
West Side News, 4, 23
West, Mae, 98
Western Electric Co., or "Bohemian U.," 71-72
Westerveldt, Dick, 144, 152
Westfall, Kay, 104-106
WGN kitchen set, 216
Whaley, Vern, 18, 73-74, 79, 112, 141, 159
Wherity, Jerry, 144, 152
White Sox team, 107-108
Wilhelmina Models, Inc., 171
Wilhelmina, 167-171
Williams, Mary Lou, 199-200
Willys Knight sedan, 7, 10
Winters, Jonathan, 22
Witter, Dean, 129-130
Wolters Air Force Base, 138
Wood, Natalie, 151

Zukerman, Eugenia, 189-190

Photographs

Good words about *Lucky George*

What a Life!

I was a paper boy in the close-in Chicago suburb of Oak Park at about the time George Kufrin clicked his first camera. Each morning, I rolled out my wagon of 128 copies of the *Tribune* and the *Times* (later the *Sun-Times),* a tabloid with a stylized picture of a vintage camera as the centerpiece of its logo. I loved these papers and knew they were as much about pictures as words. How neat, I thought, it would be to be a photographer, especially if your job called for covering exciting events and people.

So I snapped up Kufrin's book because it promised an account of his life over a period of five decades, stretching from his world travels with the Merchant Marines in WWII to his home base of Chicago, from which he hob-nobbed (camera always in hand) with world figures, entertainers we all know and love, athletes who fill our sports pages and poets, no less—like U.S. Poet Laureate Gwendolyn Brooks, head-turning writers like Mary McCarthy, and even Tarzan—five Olympic medal-winner Johnny Weissmuller. Not to mention business leaders and financial luminaries such as Dean Witter.

There's a constant sidebar to the story. It's an answer to the question, "How does an ordinary kid from an ordinary family (seemingly—his father was an outstanding sculptor) and ordinary high school end up living by his wits and excelling in this craft where it's hard to make a buck?" He seems happy-go-lucky and calls himself "Lucky George." Don't you believe it. This is a man of moxie and consummate gifts who has claimed them for his own.

Allan Cox, author
WHOA! Are They Glad You're In Their Lives?
The CEO in You
and seven other best-sellers

The 'luck' is for the reader being allowed to journey through George Kufrin's life via the gifted eye of his camera and words. We are privileged to share moments of historical intimacy, old Hollywood wow, past shakers and makers of our political, industrial and social landscape. Thanks for the memories, George...a great life—a great read!

Mary Bonnett
Artistic Director, Her Story Theater

George Kufrin photographs all of his subjects as if they possess star power. As a writer, Kufrin's take on decades of American history is spot on, like the view through the lens of his camera. Reading *Lucky George* I often laughed out loud at his self-effacing humor. A beautifully written book defining a beautiful collection of photographs.

Naomi Pringle, author
Ginga' Root Tea, an American Journey

Lucky George—Lucky for Us!

Lucky George is not only a thoroughly enjoyable collection of outstanding photographs and memories of the artist's life and work, but exceptional in that you will find yourself reading his text and looking at his photographs again and again. Kufrin strings together wonderful stories and anecdotes behind the photographs which transport us to the "scene of the crime." But there is no crime in this collection of work and stories that takes Kufrin from the Great Depression, through the U.S. Merchant Marines, to his highly inventive photos for Hawthorn Mellody milk ads (more memorable than the current "Got Milk?" ads), to his portraits of personalities, and much more. Kufrin reflects he has had a "lucky" life with all he's experienced, but he must have thought that from the beginning as is evident in his photographs through the years.

Garry McGee, author
Jean Seberg–Breathless
Doris Day: Sentimental Journey

The author of *Lucky George* quickly draws the reader in as he reveals cherished behind-the-scenes moments of his photographs—in an entertaining chronicle of famous personalities and historical milestones from the last century. George Kufrin's tales as a successful photographer bring to life some of America's finest hours. Old smoky newsrooms, blue-collar factory life in the immigrant neighborhoods, suburban sprawl, urban change, identity and the pursuit of the American dream are just some of the moments shared by Kufrin. His intriguing photos continually entice us to turn the page and read on.

Proud of his upbringing, Kufrin reveals glimpses of the old-world values he inherited from his Bohemian mother, Mae, and his Croatian father, Paul Kufrin, a successful sculptor. Written with wit and modesty, Kufrin has captured a slice of Americana and an era in Chicago that, unfortunately, will soon be forgotten.

Enjoy these pages as the man behind the lens celebrates his unforgettable journey.

Maria Dugandžić-Pašić, author
Croatians of Chicagoland
Award-winning film producer: *"They Never Walked Alone"*

What a life George Kufrin has led! I marvel at all the photographs he's made, people he has met, places he has been, and that he remembered so much of it. Obviously, he enjoyed every minute, thereby impressing the events and people on his brain. Too few people really appreciate what life deals them but *Lucky George* is a great example of someone who has.

Rebecca Dixon, associate provost, (ret.)
Northwestern University

And lucky at 17, because he was at the right place at the right time to photograph a huge coal yard fire. The *Chicago Herald American* ran the photo full page and also put it on International News Photos, the Hearst wire service. The date was Friday, October 13, 1944, the official beginning of Kufrin's free-lance career.

That career would take him across America, photographing the movers and shakers of his time. John F. Kennedy, Barry Goldwater, Dean Witter, Lena Horne, Burt Lancaster, Mary McCarthy, Nat "King" Cole, Maria Tallchief, Studs Terkel, Gwendolyn Brooks, Adlai Stevenson and Alice Neel are just a few of the hundreds of giants he has photographed over the years whom you'll meet in *Lucky George*.

With the exception of a two-year stint as a Merchant Marine during WWII and another two years as an Army photographer during Korea, Kufrin has spent his entire working life as a photographer.

His photos have appeared in *Fortune, Parade, Look, New York, New York Times, Finance, Chicago Tribune, New York News* magazine, *Chicago, DownBeat, Science, Chicago Sun-Times,* and countless Fortune 500 annual reports. In 1981, Kufrin and his wife, writer Joan Kufrin, co-authored *Uncommon Women,* published by New Century Publishers. His photographs illustrate the book.

Kufrin will discuss his lenses and cameras, film, shutter speeds and darkroom procedures but don't ask him for a statement on the philosophy of his photography.

"If I could make statements," he says, "I would be a writer. All my statements are in my pictures. The worst practice in photography is titling a picture. If the picture doesn't say it, no amount of words will."

Lightning Source UK Ltd.
Milton Keynes UK
UKHW05f1925060818
326846UK00004B/481/P